a cook's year
gregg wallace

a cook's year
gregg wallace

how to choose and cook with great ingredients

Photographs by Simon Brown

MITCHELL BEAZLEY

To Tom and Libby Wallace, a.k.a. tip-face and lob-head.
Rugby, netball, sulks and tantrums. Daddy will always love you.

A COOK'S YEAR

First published in Great Britain in 2008 by Mitchell Beazley,
an imprint of Octopus Publishing Group Ltd,
2–4 Heron Quays, London E14 4JP
An Hachette Livre Company
www.octopusbooks.co.uk

ISBN-13: 978 1 84533 327 0

A CIP record for this book is available from the British Library

Set in Tradegothic

Colour reproduction by Sang Choy, China
Printed and bound in China by Toppan Printing Company Limited, China

Commissioning Editor Rebecca Spry
Project Editor Leanne Bryan
Editor Susan Fleming
Proofreader Alison Leach
Art Director Tim Foster
Designer Nicky Collings
Home Economist Zed Palmer
Prop Stylist Isabel De Cordova
Senior Production Controller Lucy Carter
Photographer Simon Brown
Indexer John Noble

CONTENTS

Spring 22

Spring ingredients • Lamb • Veal • Monkfish •
Scallops • Asparagus • Peas • Sprouting broccoli •
Spring greens • New and salad potatoes • Rhubarb

Summer 68

Summer ingredients • Sea bass • Crab • Swiss chard •
Broad beans • Tomatoes • Baby carrots • Rocket •
Cherries • Strawberries • Raspberries

Autumn 114

Autumn ingredients • Duck • Pheasant • Partridge •
Cod • Prawns • Sweetcorn • Beetroot • Apples •
Plums • Blackberries

Winter 162

Winter ingredients • Venison • Grouse • Mussels •
Smoked haddock • Potatoes • Carrots • Parsnips •
Cabbage • Leeks • Pears

INTRODUCTION

This book has taken me more than a year to write. For the most part it has been a labour of love. The cooking was great; I love the time I spend in the kitchen. Alongside my cooking utensils, I have a list of essentials: a radio, a CD player, a big stack of CDs by artists who are dead, and a decent bottle of wine. But a book such as this is not all about recipes. I also share a lifetime of accumulated information about seasonal eating.

'Seasonal' and 'local' are the buzz words of people who work in the food industry. And cooking seasonally is delightful. There's always a new culinary present waiting just around the corner; always something to look forward to. It's like having a couple of hundred little birthday celebrations each year! But how are we supposed to know which foods are in season when? Supermarkets stock most produce all year round and none of us, however great our knowledge of food, can be expected to be an expert on fish, meat, fruit, salads and vegetables. This guide lists all of the major British ingredients along with their seasons. I didn't realize, until I made an extensive list, what a mammoth task I had set myself. We have an abundance of truly wonderful natural foods on these islands.

I've been in the food business all my working life. Everything I do is about food. I write about it in magazines, I talk about it on the radio, and I eat it constantly on the television. Many of you, I suspect, will know me from *MasterChef*, where I'm given the unusual title of 'ingredients expert', without any word of explanation as to why I should hold this lofty title. Well, I'm a greengrocer. I started at Covent Garden Market, and am now based at Secretts Farm in Surrey. I have supplied virtually all (and this is no idle boast) of the best chefs in London with fresh fruit and vegetables. Over the years, I've spent a huge amount of time in their kitchens, and it is these talented people that I would like to thank for the knowledge I have. They have introduced me to the best ingredients and taught me what to look for and how to handle them. Between seeing the best produce in its raw state in their kitchens and eating it cooked to perfection in their restaurants, I've had a hugely enjoyable 25-year apprenticeship in the best of British food.

Over the years I've built good friendships with like-minded people who deliver quality fish and meats. With a restaurant industry as big and diverse as that in London, there are surprisingly few suppliers of high-quality foods, and we all know each other well. Throughout this book I have enlisted the help of these experts in their particular field. Above all, I'd like to mention Gary Bentley – I know of no finer butcher; Mitch Tonks of *FishWorks* – a hugely passionate man and an old friend; and Steve, my local fishmonger in Whitstable – a top bloke who has been a real help. Thank you to all three.

Finally, I want to discuss the recipes. I've picked my favourite ingredients from each season and had real fun cooking with them all. I've gone over them with a fine tooth comb to make sure they work perfectly. I'm not a chef; these recipes are simply the dishes I most love to eat. They are home recipes – dishes that I make for my family or friends. I hope that you get as much enjoyment from them as I do.

SEASONAL GUIDE

○ IN SEASON ● BEST

FISH	Jan	Feb	Mar	Apr	May	Jun	Jul	Aug	Sep	Oct	Nov	Dec
Bream	○	○	○	○	○	●	●	●	○	○	○	○
Brill	●	●	○	○	○	●	●	●	●	●	●	●
Cod	○	○	○	○	○	○	○	○	●	●	●	○
Coley	●	●	●	●	●	●	●	●	●	●	●	●
Crab	●	●	●	●	●	●	●	●	●	●	●	●
Dover sole	○	○	○	○	○	●	●	●	○	○	○	○
Eel	○	○	○	○	○	○	○	○	●	●	●	○
Grey mullet	○	○	○	○	○	○	○	○	●	●	●	○
Gurnard	○	○	○	○	○	●	●	●	○	○	○	○
Haddock	●	●	○	○	○	○	○	○	○	○	○	●
Hake	●	●	○	○	○	○	○	○	○	○	○	●
Halibut	○	○	○	○	○	○	○	○	●	●	●	○
Herring	●	●	○	○	○	○	○	○	○	○	○	●
John Dory	●	●	●	●	●	●	●	●	●	●	●	●
Langoustine	○	○	●	●	●	●	●	●	●	●	●	○
Lemon sole	○	○	○	○	○	●	●	●	○	○	○	○
Lobster	○	○	●	●	●	●	●	●	○	○	○	○
Mackerel	○	○	○	○	○	●	●	●	○	○	○	○
Monkfish	○	○	●	●	●	○	○	○	○	○	○	○
Mussel	●	●	○	○	○	○	○	○	○	○	○	●
Oyster	●	●	○	○	○	○	○	○	●	●	●	●
Plaice	○	○	●	●	●	●	●	●	●	●	●	○
Pollack	○	○	○	○	○	●	●	●	○	○	○	○
Prawn	○	○	○	○	○	●	●	●	●	●	●	○
Salmon	○	○	○	○	○	●	●	●	○	○	○	○
Scallop	○	○	●	●	●	○	○	○	○	○	○	○
Sea bass	○	○	○	○	○	●	●	●	○	○	○	○
Sea trout	○	○	○	○	○	●	●	●	○	○	○	○

	Jan	Feb	Mar	Apr	May	Jun	Jul	Aug	Sep	Oct	Nov	Dec	
	○	○	○	○	○	●	●	●	○	○	○	○	Shrimp
	●	●	●	●	●	●	●	●	○	○	○	●	Skate
	●	●	○	○	○	○	○	○	●	●	●	●	Sprat
	○	○	○	○	○	●	●	●	○	○	○	○	Turbot
	●	●	○	○	○	○	○	○	○	○	○	●	Whitebait
	●	●	○	○	○	○	○	○	○	○	○	●	Whiting
	○	○	○	○	○	●	●	●	○	○	○	○	Winkle

MEAT

	Jan	Feb	Mar	Apr	May	Jun	Jul	Aug	Sep	Oct	Nov	Dec	
	○	○	○	●	●	●	●	●	●	●	●	○	Lamb
	○	○	●	●	●	○	○	○	○	○	○	○	Veal

GAME

	Jan	Feb	Mar	Apr	May	Jun	Jul	Aug	Sep	Oct	Nov	Dec	
	●	○	○	○	○	○	○	○	●	●	●	●	Duck
	●	○	○	○	○	○	○	●	●	●	●	●	Grouse
	●	●	○	○	○	○	○	○	●	●	●	●	Partridge
	●	●	○	○	○	○	○	○	●	●	●	●	Pheasant
	●	●	○	○	○	●	●	●	●	●	●	●	Venison

VEGETABLES

	Jan	Feb	Mar	Apr	May	Jun	Jul	Aug	Sep	Oct	Nov	Dec	
	○	○	○	●	●	●	○	○	○	○	○	○	Asparagus
	○	○	○	●	●	●	●	○	○	○	○	○	Baby carrot
	●	●	○	○	○	●	●	●	●	●	●	●	Beetroot
	○	○	○	●	●	●	●	●	●	●	○	○	Bok choi
	○	○	○	○	○	○	○	○	●	●	●	○	Borlotti bean
	○	○	○	○	●	●	●	●	●	○	○	○	Broad bean
	●	●	●	○	○	○	○	○	○	○	○	●	Brussels sprout
	●	●	○	○	○	○	○	○	○	○	●	●	Brussels top
	●	●	●	○	○	○	○	○	○	●	●	●	Cabbage
	●	○	○	○	○	●	●	●	●	●	●	○	Calabrese
	●	●	○	○	○	●	○	●	●	●	●	○	Cannellini bean

	Jan	Feb	Mar	Apr	May	Jun	Jul	Aug	Sep	Oct	Nov	Dec
Cardoon	○	○	○	○	○	○	○	○	◐	●	●	◐
Carrot	◐	◐	◐	◐	●	●	●	●	●	●	●	●
Cauliflower	○	○	◐	●	●	●	●	●	●	●	◐	◐
Cavolo nero	●	●	○	○	○	○	○	○	◐	●	●	●
Celeriac	◐	◐	◐	○	○	○	○	○	◐	◐	●	●
Celery	●	◐	○	○	○	○	○	○	◐	●	●	●
Chilli	○	○	○	○	○	○	○	◐	●	●	◐	○
Courgette	○	○	○	○	○	○	●	●	●	●	○	○
Courgette flower	○	○	○	○	○	◐	●	●	●	○	○	○
Fennel	○	○	○	○	○	○	○	●	●	●	○	○
French bean	○	○	○	○	○	○	●	●	◐	◐	○	○
Garlic	○	○	○	○	●	●	●	●	●	◐	○	○
Globe artichoke	○	○	○	○	◐	◐	●	●	●	●	○	○
Horseradish	○	○	●	●	○	○	○	○	○	○	○	○
Jerusalem artichoke	●	●	◐	○	○	○	○	○	○	○	○	○
Leek	●	●	●	◐	○	○	○	◐	◐	●	●	●
Mangetout	○	○	○	○	○	◐	●	●	●	○	○	○
Marrow	○	○	○	○	○	○	○	●	●	●	●	○
Mushroom	●	●	●	●	●	●	●	●	●	●	●	●
New and salad potatoes	○	○	○	○	◐	●	●	●	○	○	○	○
Onion	●	●	◐	◐	◐	◐	○	●	●	●	●	●
Parsnip	●	◐	◐	○	○	○	○	○	◐	●	●	●
Pea	○	○	○	○	○	●	●	●	◐	○	○	○
Pepper	○	○	○	○	○	○	○	◐	●	●	◐	○
Potato	●	●	◐	◐	◐	◐	◐	●	●	●	●	◐
Runner bean	○	○	○	○	○	○	◐	●	●	◐	○	○
Salsify	◐	◐	○	○	○	○	○	●	●	●	●	◐
Samphire	○	○	○	○	◐	●	●	◐	○	○	○	○
Sea kale	○	○	◐	◐	●	●	◐	○	○	○	○	○
Shallot	●	●	○	○	○	○	○	○	●	●	●	●
Spinach	◐	◐	◐	◐	◐	○	●	●	●	◐	◐	●

	Jan	Feb	Mar	Apr	May	Jun	Jul	Aug	Sep	Oct	Nov	Dec	
	●	●	●	●	◐	○	○	○	○	○	◐	●	Spring greens
	◐	◐	●	●	◐	○	○	○	○	○	○	◐	Sprouting broccoli
	○	○	○	○	○	●	●	●	●	○	○	○	Sugar snap
	○	○	○	○	○	○	◐	●	◐	○	○	○	Summer squash
	●	●	◐	○	○	○	○	◐	◐	○	●	●	Swede
	○	○	○	○	○	○	◐	◐	●	◐	○	○	Sweetcorn
	○	○	○	○	○	○	◐	●	●	●	●	◐	Swiss chard
	●	◐	○	○	○	○	○	○	◐	◐	○	●	Turnip
	○	○	○	○	○	○	○	○	◐	●	●	◐	Winter squash

FRUIT

	Jan	Feb	Mar	Apr	May	Jun	Jul	Aug	Sep	Oct	Nov	Dec	
	◐	◐	○	○	○	○	○	◐	●	●	●	●	Apple
	○	○	○	○	○	○	◐	●	●	○	○	○	Blackberry
	○	○	○	○	○	○	●	●	●	○	○	○	Blueberry
	○	○	○	●	●	●	◐	○	○	○	○	○	Cherry
	○	○	○	○	○	●	●	○	○	○	○	○	Currant
	○	○	○	○	○	●	●	◐	○	○	○	○	Gooseberry
	○	○	○	○	○	○	○	○	○	●	●	○	Medlar
	●	◐	○	○	○	○	○	○	●	●	●	●	Pear
	○	○	○	○	○	○	◐	●	●	○	○	○	Plum
	○	○	○	○	○	○	○	○	●	●	◐	○	Quince
	○	○	○	○	○	○	●	●	◐	●	●	○	Raspberry
	●	●	●	●	●	●	◐	○	○	○	○	○	Rhubarb
	○	○	○	○	○	●	●	◐	◐	○	○	○	Strawberry
	○	○	○	○	○	◐	●	●	●	●	◐	○	Tomato

SALADS

	Jan	Feb	Mar	Apr	May	Jun	Jul	Aug	Sep	Oct	Nov	Dec	
	●	●	●	◐	○	○	○	○	○	◐	●	●	Chicory
	○	○	○	○	○	●	●	●	◐	○	○	○	Cos
	○	○	○	○	○	◐	◐	●	●	◐	○	○	Cucumber
	○	○	◐	●	●	○	○	○	○	○	○	○	Dandelion

	Jan	Feb	Mar	Apr	May	Jun	Jul	Aug	Sep	Oct	Nov	Dec
Frisée	○	○	○	○	○	●	●	●	◐	○	○	○
Gem/little gem	○	○	○	◐	◐	●	●	●	◐	○	○	○
Iceberg	○	○	○	○	○	●	●	●	◐	○	○	○
Lollo rosso	○	○	○	●	●	●	●	●	●	○	○	○
Oakleaf	○	○	○	●	●	●	●	●	◐	○	○	○
Radicchio	●	●	●	○	○	○	○	○	◐	●	●	●
Rocket	●	●	●	●	●	●	●	●	●	●	●	●
Spring onion	○	○	◐	●	●	●	●	●	◐	○	○	○
Watercress	○	○	●	●	●	◐	◐	◐	◐	●	●	○

HERBS

	Jan	Feb	Mar	Apr	May	Jun	Jul	Aug	Sep	Oct	Nov	Dec
Basil	○	○	○	○	○	◐	●	●	●	○	○	○
Chervil	○	○	○	◐	●	●	●	●	◐	○	○	○
Coriander	○	○	○	○	◐	●	●	●	◐	○	○	○
Dill	○	○	○	○	◐	●	●	●	◐	○	○	○
Mint	○	○	◐	●	●	●	●	●	◐	◐	○	○
Oregano	○	○	◐	●	●	●	●	●	◐	◐	○	○
Parsley	○	○	◐	●	●	●	●	●	●	●	◐	○
Rosemary	◐	◐	◐	●	●	●	●	●	●	●	◐	●
Sage	◐	◐	◐	●	●	●	●	●	●	◐	◐	◐
Tarragon	○	○	◐	●	●	●	●	●	◐	◐	○	○
Thyme	●	●	◐	●	●	●	●	●	◐	◐	◐	●

NUTS

	Jan	Feb	Mar	Apr	May	Jun	Jul	Aug	Sep	Oct	Nov	Dec
Chestnut	●	◐	○	○	○	○	○	○	◐	●	●	●
Hazelnut	○	○	○	○	○	○	○	●	●	○	○	○
Walnut	○	○	○	○	○	○	○	○	◐	●	●	○

COOKING WITH MEAT THROUGH THE SEASONS

I've covered all the major seasonal lines in this book, but meat is a tricky one. Apart from veal and lamb, which we associate with spring, other beasts can be eaten all year round. So, I'm going to cover chicken, beef and pork in this section rather than put them in a seasonal chapter.

I give information on different cuts of meat. Basically, the spring and summer seasons lend themselves to the quicker and lighter cooking of meat – grilling, frying, stir-frying and, although in this country it slightly frightens me, barbecuing. The winter lends itself to slower cooking, such as roasts and stews. You need to choose your cuts accordingly.

VEAL

Well, here's a tricky subject, and one fraught with much emotion. It was the Normans who first brought the tradition of killing young animals to Britain. The hearty Anglo-Saxons thought it a waste of what would grow up to be a much bigger, meat-giving beast. There is no real British tradition of veal, although it is becoming very popular now. That said, there still is no denying that veal is expensive and a luxury.

No-one can condone the treatment once traditionally associated with veal calves. Very small calves were taken from their mothers, kept in dark pens in which they couldn't move around and were fed milk supplements, all to keep their flesh pale and white. They were slaughtered at eight to twelve weeks. Not surprisingly, a lot of potential customers didn't like this custom. Now we are much more humane, and the babies are kept with their mothers, they live and feed naturally for up to four to six months (the same as a lamb or piglet), and their flesh is pinker as a result. Many people in the world still believe the whiter veal to be superior and turn their noses up at anything with a hint of pink. I disagree. What is now known as 'rose' veal is very flavoursome meat. At least with pink-tinged meat you know that the calf has led a more natural existence.

Veal is a firm, tender and creamy meat, with very little fat and no marbling. Actually it does have fat running through it, but it's so fine it's virtually impossible to see. The meat of milk-fed veal is white. What you want, if like me you have a conscience, is grass-fed veal, which is pink or rose-coloured. (Veal has to be pink, never red; red is too old.) Avoid any cut that has a tinge of grey or brown, which is a sign that the meat is going stale. The fat should be white. If there is too much fat on the meat, or you can clearly see marbling, the animal has been forcibly over-fed. The lack of fat can mean the veal is dry when cooking, so it will need the help of extra oil or butter.

I have a particular fondness for calf's brains, which have a lovely soft and slightly springy texture. Not many restaurants serve them these days. My butcher can get them, but they're in trays of twelve, and even I can't manage twelve calf brains at a sitting!

LAMB

Lamb is definitely, definitely my favourite meat. There's lots of fat on this beast, which keeps it nice and moist when cooking.

There are different laws throughout Europe regarding the age at which you can slaughter a lamb. In Spain, milk-fed lamb is a delicacy. This is a lamb that is slaughtered while it is still weaning. It's not for me. Its flesh is very soft and milky, but I like my lambs a little more robust.

A sheep should only be sold as lamb if it's aged between four months and one year. From one year to two years it is known as 'hogget'. This is a particular favourite of mine. I like the stronger flavour that the ageing brings. After two years it becomes 'mutton'. Nothing wrong with mutton, it just needs a bit more cooking. Lamb, of course, is pink; hogget is redder; and mutton is deep red.

Because of the high fat content on a lamb, it can stand longer cooking then most meat. The perfect colour on cooked meat is a matter of personal choice. I serve mine with a hint of pink. As I've said, all that fat will keep the meat very moist indeed.

Because of the fat, lamb can take strong flavours. Garlic, thyme and rosemary are perfect accompaniments for the beast. And please serve it with mint sauce!

We are blessed on these islands with lots of rain, which means many green things grow naturally in our fields and meadows. The lamb's ability to eat anything green means it can survive quite happily on nearly barren land, which, in turn, means that the lambing industry has not been subjected to the horrors of intensive farming. There are so many sheep in Britain that every decent butcher should have locally reared meat.

CHICKEN

Come on, who doesn't love a roast chicken? My teenage son Tom would walk barefoot across coals to get at a chicken and its soft, moist, flavoursome meat. A steaming bird at your dinner table is a thing of joy. A roasted chicken suits any time of year. Don't forget, you can always cook it and serve it once it's cooled if the weather is really hot.

Buying quality chicken is a problem. There are numerous issues. You would think you were safe with 'free-range', wouldn't you? But 'free-range' doesn't necessarily mean the chickens have been fluttering all over a grassy meadow. You have to ask the butcher lots of questions about his source. Take 'maize-fed' for example: this can mean that the chicken is still reared intensively and disgustingly, but fed on 'some' cornmeal. There are also huge amounts of chickens flown to Britain from countries outside of the EU. Once these birds have been brought to a registered abattoir, they can then be labelled 'English'. I ask you, how can I, a man living on the Kent coast, find out what conditions my chicken from South-East Asia was reared in?

I urge you, please, to spend the extra money and buy organic chicken. I don't want to list the horror stories of intensive chicken farming, but you have probably heard some of them already. It's the texture and the flavour you get from a well-bred, happy bird that, once tasted, makes buying anything else seem ridiculous. I know they seem to be so much more money, but it is

THIS WEEK
WILD FALLOW
ORGANIC PORK
CHICKEN NUGGETS
MUTTON
FRANGE DUCK
PERTHSHIRE BEEF

worth it. I can't believe how cheap chicken has become. A little while ago I was amazed to see a whole cooked chicken for £1.50 in my supermarket. I had to buy it just to check it out and I was delighted when the thing turned out to be completely hideous: tough and, apart from the herbs it was cooked in, virtually tasteless.

Poussins These are baby chickens, slaughtered at around four weeks old. The meat is very tender, but they most certainly don't have the flavour of a well brought up, completely organic chicken.

BEEF

There's something very British about roast beef. Soft, pink meat and horseradish on the dinner table brings the broadest of grins to my weather-beaten face. I think it's worth having a lot of people over for Sunday lunch just so you can serve the biggest piece of beef possible.

When shopping for beef there are a number of things you should look for. The first is the colour: it should be deep red, not pinky red. Ask the butcher how long the meat has been hung. Well-hung meat is juicy and tasty. Hung meat shrinks, thereby losing weight. So, well-hung meat will be better but more expensive. It should have hung for between a week and a month.

The meat should look dry, not wet or sweaty. Touch it if you can; it should feel sticky, firm and springy. Push it with your finger; the indentation should stay.

Marbling is a term most people have heard of. The marbling effect in beef is caused by very thin, almost vein-like lines of soft white fat running through the cut. This gives the meat a soft and succulent texture. Good beef also has a generous layer of outer fat. You need fat to keep the flesh moist during cooking and, as it melts, you can use it to baste your joint. You don't have to eat all the fat, but you do need to cook with it.

Fillet This is the underside of the sirloin and for years has been much prized. My friend and companion on *MasterChef*, John Torode, is annoyed with the English obsession with fillet, reasoning that this piece of meat does hardly any work on the animal and therefore lacks flavour. Anyone who has visited the top floor of Smiths of Smithfield will realize John knows a thing or two about beef.

Fore-rib This is the baby for me. It is the back of the beast, just behind its forelegs. Many cuts come from the fore-rib and it's brilliant for roasting. It has plenty of fat and the bone running through it helps conduct heat when cooking and keeps the meat moist. It is arguably the most flavoursome part of the animal and it is from the fore-rib that the rib-eye steak is cut.

Rump This cut is the curving end of a cow's back. It can be chewy if you don't get really good meat. When it is good, it makes excellent steaks for frying or grilling.

Silverside This is the back of the thigh and gets its name from the shiny, almost silver covering. Silverside is a pair of quite tough muscles. It's best used for long, slow cooking such as stewing.

Skirt This is a group of muscles from inside the beast. The cut is low on fat and therefore quite lean. It is best used in long slow-cooked dishes.

Topside This is a long, inner muscle, on the beast's thigh. It is perfect for long roasting.

PORK

For me, pork represents soft meat and, above all, crackling. Who doesn't love crackling? My daughter, Libby, would even forego a game of netball, I think, as long as she could get her hands on a good bit of crackling. The thing to remember if you want good crackling is not to allow any liquid to get near it; it has to be completely dry – any liquid at all and you have instant leather.

Too many people overcook pork. My good mate Gary Bentley is an excellent butcher, and that is his favourite moan. He has demonstrated to me more than once that pork can be served pink. Study the pig. It doesn't move around that much, does it? Well, not enough for its meat to get tough anyway.

All of this beast can be roasted. In fact, the only bit of a pig you can't eat is its squeak! Avoid wet-looking pork, or waxy-looking fat and, when choosing pork, stick your nose up to it and have a good smell. If it has any kind of smell at all, it's going stale.

Belly A pig has an extraordinarily long belly and there are nice thin layers of fat between the layers of meat on this cut, which makes overcooking it virtually impossible. It also gives the best quality crackling.

Chaps These are the cheeks cut away from the head of the pig. They are very soft and succulent.

Hock This is the first joint of the front leg, and contains lots of sinew, gristle and bone. It needs a lot of slow cooking to melt down all that sinew.

Loin This is the long back and ribs of the pig. The front bit is the fore-loin; the middle bit the middle-loin; and at the end, the chump. All of the loin can be bought cut up as chops, and all of the loin can be boned and rolled to make a very good joint for roasting.

Spare ribs These are trimmed from the belly, usually at the thicker end. They have to be eaten with your fingers. The bones act as natural handles with which to properly enjoy the soft meat.

Suckling pig This pig is slaughtered between three and eight weeks old. The meat is beautiful and soft, and it's pure theatre to serve it whole at the table.

Tenderloin This is the most delicate, but also the most lean part of the loin, and it can dry very easily with just a hint of overcooking.

Trotters These are a particular favourite of mine as they can be stuffed with all sorts of goodies. But there's not much meat on a trotter; it's all skin and sinew. For trotters to become soft and flavoursome they need to be cooked for virtually 24 hours. Any less, and the result is a disgusting rubberiness.

Spring

Spring ingredients

COLEY This is a member of the cod family. It doesn't have a great flavour, and most of it ends up as cat food, which is a shame because it's a good, cheap fish, as firm as a cod but with less flavour. It's great in pies and just as good in fishcakes. I think people don't buy it because of its unattractive grey flesh. It does turn white when you cook it, and it goes a brilliant white if you rub it with lemon first.

CRAB (*see* page 70 and recipes, pages 82–85)

JOHN DORY This armour-plated fish looks almost prehistoric. It has long, sharp fins that are really tough. I've pierced many a finger while handling a John Dory. The fins and big brown spots like a thumbprint in the middle of the fish make the John Dory easily recognizable. This fish is gold in colour but loses that colour as soon as you land it. If you are lucky enough to find a John Dory with a hint of gold, you have a very fresh fish indeed. The flesh is white, firm and succulent, and comes away from the bone very easily, but because it's so thin and it has all that armour, there is a heck of a lot of waste and the fillets are very small.

LANGOUSTINE The langoustine is a crustacean with many aliases, the most popular of which are Dublin Bay prawn, Norway lobster and scampi. Scampi used to be cheap until somebody started selling the fish whole with the heads and tails intact and renamed them 'langoustine'. Now they are highly prized and hugely expensive. I still like to refer to them as scampi.

Once caught, langoustines deteriorate alarmingly quickly and they are nearly always sold ready cooked. It's up to you how you cook them. You can view one and prepare it as either a big shrimp or a small lobster, although I find too much liquid in cooking makes them a bit soggy and tasteless. My old mate William Black recommends roasting them whole in the oven for no longer than 5 minutes.

LOBSTER What is it with me and crustaceans? I just adore them, the lobster best of all. So much sweet flesh, which demands chewing and savouring carefully. Lobsters are also so much fun to eat, hammering and cracking away with your pincers.

What you want is an old lobster. When they're young, they shed their shells regularly. As they age, they shed them less, so older lobsters have more time to fill out their shells with flesh. Look out for big tough shells, preferably with barnacles attached. When you pick them up they should feel very heavy; lobsters kept in captivity lose weight quickly. Please make sure their claws are bound before you do so, or you may end up as the lobster's lunch, instead of vice versa! Always buy your lobsters alive. They should move around. They are usually a bluey-green/black, and only go red when cooked. Many people are squeamish about throwing a live creature into boiling water and I can understand this. Research suggests that the most humane way of killing a lobster is to put it in a plastic bag with holes and place it in the freezer. Apparently it just dozes off to sleep and slowly loses consciousness.

MONKFISH (*see* recipes, pages 38–41) I've got no idea why this great big fish is named after a monk, and neither has anybody else I speak to. Many people around the world know it as the 'angler fish'. The monkfish is carnivorous and it gets its name 'angler' because of the way it hunts. The smooth grey or brown skin means it can sit, perfectly camouflaged, on the sea bed and dangle a little flexible rod that protrudes from its head. Smaller fish are attracted by this and, as soon as they get near, wallop! The monkfish has them in that huge mouth and between its amazingly sharp teeth.

The monkfish is an ugly beast. It's rare to see a whole one. Its disproportionately large head makes up 50 per cent of its weight. Nobody wants to buy the head so it's always the tail you see in the shop, and this is one of the best pieces of fish you can buy.

PLAICE This is a flat fish with red spots on top and white spots underneath. It's a favourite in fish and chip shops as its flesh is soft and mild in flavour. If you don't get a fresh plaice, it will taste of hardly anything. This is why it is often eaten in a seasoned batter. I have enjoyed this fish grilled, but it's got to be really fresh, when its red spots will be vivid, like little ink stains. If not, batter it!

SCALLOP (*see* recipes, pages 42–45) Always buy scallops in the shell and eat them that day. Scallops in their shell are a mild grey colour, surrounded by an orange roe. Only scallops that have been washed turn white, and when they are washed to whiteness, they fill up with water and become puffy.

To remove a scallop from its shell use a strong flat blade to prise the shell apart, then slide the knife under the scallop and it will come away easily. Quickly rinse under cold water and remove the transparent membrane. Our cousins in the US discard the roe – heaven knows why; I think it's the best part. Diver-caught scallops are expensive, but nearly always better. Dredging the sea-bed for them damages the shells and can fill them with sand or grit.

SKATE I love this fish! That beautiful, pinky-white, sweet flesh comes away from the skeleton with the lightest of touches from your knife. The skate has no bones: its frame is completely cartilage.

It's rare to see a whole skate in a fishmongers – we usually see only the wings, which is a shame because the knobs from the tail are cheap and very good. Don't buy skate just caught. They are really tough when they are fresh and are better eaten two or three days out of the sea. Sniff your skate, and if you get the merest hint of ammonia, discard it. Many a fishmonger will tell you the ammonia will disappear in cooking, but this is rubbish.

LAMB (*see* recipes, pages 30–33 and Cooking with meat through the seasons, page 16)

VEAL (*see* recipes, pages 34–37 and Cooking with meat through the seasons, page 15)

ASPARAGUS (*see* recipes, pages 46–49) Asparagus is expensive for a number of reasons, mostly because of the difficulty in harvesting. The delicate spears defy machine harvesting; every spear has to be cut by hand. It also needs a lot of land to grow on, with at least 30cm (1ft) between each spear. The price is also bumped up by the fact that when you sow asparagus you have virtually nothing to pick for at least two years. Then you will only get spears for, at most, three seasons. This means that a field of asparagus is unproductive for about 50 per cent of the time.

Only Brits and Italians eat asparagus green. The rest of Europe eat theirs white. To achieve a white spear you have to blanch it. This means as it grows you have to pile the earth up around it to keep the sunlight off.

CARROT (*see* page 165 and recipes, pages 186–189; *see also* Baby Carrot, page 71, and recipes, pages 96–97)

CAULIFLOWER The cauli is an amazing veg. Its a brassica, and belongs to the same family as cabbages. What delights me about it are those little white florets. Incredibly, these are flower buds just ready to flower, but they develop no further.

Caulis needn't be whiter than white. They come in many shades, from bright white all the way to yellow. A white head with yellow bits is wrong, but a creamy yellow colour all over is likely to be a variety of just that colour. As long as the heads are tight and snap easily without too much bending, and as long as the florets are free of 'rust spots', you have a fresh cauli.

LEEK (*see* page 165; *see also* recipes, pages 196–199)

MANGETOUT *Mange tout* is French for 'eat all'. I would translate it as 'don't bother with the silly little buggers'! Once, mangetouts were immature pea pods. Now they are a variety all of their own. Quite how and why this has come about, I have no idea. They are virtually tasteless and have the texture of rubber.

MUSHROOMS

I'm discussing cultivated mushrooms here, not wild. You will find wild mushrooms in the autumn and early winter, although growers are now cultivating some mushrooms that used to be wild. The two most successful ex-wild types are shiitake and oyster. Shiitake is meaty, oyster is fairly flavourless.

The three most popular cultivated mushrooms are actually one variety: button, cup and flat are the same mushroom in different stages of development.

The button is the mushroom at baby stage. Its head has just popped through the earth and it is soft enough to be eaten raw, but has virtually no flavour. The cup is the mushroom in its teenage years. It is up to six times the size of the button, but is still a closed ball. At this point, flavour is still developing. The open cup is the next stage on. From above, it looks like a cup, but if you turn it upside down you will notice the gills, which are turning brown. The flat or field is the mushroom completely developed. It is the shape of a frisbee, soft white on top with dark brown, almost grey, gills underneath. This, to me, is a proper mushroom with all the flavour.

The Portobello is big in size and flavour, and a variety all of its own. It can be up to four times the size of a normal flat mushroom and has a brown flaky, soft top. The chestnut is an immature Portobello. If you want a round or flat mushroom, choose this; it has more flavour than any other mushroom of its size.

NEW AND SALAD POTATOES

(*see* recipes, pages 60–63; *see also* Potatoes, page 166, and recipes, pages 182–185) Everybody has a pet hate and mine is the mis-identification of new potatoes. Everyone thinks any little potato is a new potato, but this is wrong! The skin of a new potato flakes away when you rub your thumb across it – and the best new potatoes are Jersey Royals. If it doesn't flake, it's a salad potato.

Salad potatoes are perfect little boilers or roasters, and are nearly always waxy. My favourites are Belle de Fontenay, Ratte, Pink Fir Apple and Charlotte.

ONIONS

The onion is the grandfather of the allium family, which includes chives, spring onions, garlic, leeks and shallots.

A guide to brown-skinned onions is their size. The smaller they are, the stronger they are. Spanish onions are the biggest, and are useful if you have to prepare onions in bulk, but they are full of water.

Nearly all onions are white-fleshed, but the white onion has a white skin and its flesh is mild and sweet. The pickling onion is a round marble-sized brown-skinned onion. Pearl onions are tiny little white, sweet onions. These are the ones you get served as canapés in cocktail bars. Silverskin onions are similar to pearl onions, just slightly bigger. Grelot is a mature, bulbous, spring onion. Its head looks and feels too heavy for its stem. It is not mild or soft enough to eat raw unless sliced thinly. It is a bunched, milder, cooking onion. The red onion, sometimes called the Italian onion, is mild and sweet.

PEAS

(*see* recipes, pages 50–53) I recommend that you get peas very fresh indeed; ideally less than one day old. In fact, grow them yourself. Don't bother buying them, because after one day peas harden and lose their flavour. They deteriorate quicker than any other vegetable I know, and often you are better off with canned or frozen peas. Size is also important. The smaller they are, the sweeter they are. A green cannonball is no use to anybody.

I feel obliged to clarify the *petits pois* confusion. In France, any small peas are called *petits pois*. In England, we used to give the name to the smallest and youngest peas. Nowadays, *petits pois* are a completely different dwarf variety, one that remains tiny even when fully matured.

POTATOES

(*see* page 166 and recipes, pages 182–185; *see also* New and salad potatoes, this page, and recipes, pages 60–63)

SEA KALE

Sea kale is a kind of wild cabbage, although it is really a member of the mustard family. Although some people force it under pots, it is predominantly a wild plant found near the sea. It has thin celery-like stalks and leaves that are small in comparison with the stalk. I suggest you cook the leaves and the stems separately. The stems should be boiled in salted water for around 10 minutes. The leaves, cooked the same way, will be ready in under 2 minutes.

If you can get forced sea kale from a trader, the leaves are naturally yellow with a purple edge. If you pick your kale wild, make sure it is completely white. The wild sea kale pushes its way up through the sandy soil, getting no sunlight as it grows. This lack of sunlight, or blanching, gives the kale a mild flavour. Any plant that pushes itself free of the soil early will have colour. Avoid these specimens, as they are extremely bitter and virtually inedible.

SHALLOTS
Shallots come in two types: banana and round. It is impossible to say what difference there is in flavour, as you have to consider the varieties of each type and the length of time they have been stored. A banana-shaped shallot is easier to peel, chop or slice because it is four times the size of its round cousin.

The major difference between a shallot and an onion is the bulb. They are both alliums, but when there is a single bulb it's an onion; when there are two it's a shallot.

Most people I speak to are unsure when to use an onion or a shallot. I have stacks of cookery books in my kitchen and the advice I get from them is conflicting. Some say shallots are milder, some stronger, and some even claim the shallot has the strength of the onion without the smell. What is true, though, is that when a shallot is browned, its taste is very bitter, unlike an onion. So the shallot should always be softened, never browned.

SPINACH
I don't know what spinach did for Popeye, but it does wonders for me. Those soft leaves with that mild iron taste delight me.

Spinach is easy to prepare and cook. Wash well, discard the thicker stalks, and put in a pan with some butter. I never add water to the pan. I make sure I toss the spinach constantly whilst cooking. The leaves will shed so much liquid that they never burn. What you have to do is turn the heat up high towards the end to get rid of all the liquid.

Because the spinach releases so much liquid, the leaves shrink. Consider this when cooking it. One minute you will have a pot spilling over with fresh green leaves, the next minute you will have a tiny bit of cooked spinach at the bottom.

SPRING GREENS (see recipes, pages 56–59)
Spring greens are hard to pin down and classify as one type of brassica. They can come from a number of the lighter green cabbages that appear at this time of year (which include the variety Hispi). These are usually cone-shaped, coming to a point, surrounded by big floppy leaves. They are not as dense as most headed cabbages – the ones that form themselves into tight balls.

SPROUTING BROCCOLI (see recipes, pages 54–55)
Whenever I mention broccoli to people they think of the calabrese variety (see page 118). This is the big boxing glove broccoli with the short thick stem and the big bud. Calabrese is a relatively new hybrid from the south of Italy, while sprouting broccoli is the original and by far the better brassica.

SUGAR SNAP
The sugar snap was once a pea pod harvested immature. These days, it's a separate variety. Pea green, crunchy, and very sweet, the whole thing may be eaten. There is only one thing to look for, and that is the stringy bit running along the length of one side. If this has formed, take the time to remove it. It's a tricky job but not as tricky as picking green string from your teeth after a meal.

FRUIT

RHUBARB (see recipes, pages 64–67)
I like to see rhubarb growing at the farm. It looks like an alien. I particularly like the way those thick stems support such huge leaves, which always grow over to protect the crown.

It's difficult to know whether to classify rhubarb as a fruit or a vegetable. Experts have always had it sitting, albeit uncomfortably, with the vegetables, but in 1947 a US court ruled it a fruit, as nobody could come up with any evidence to show that it wasn't always used as a dessert.

The English introduced rhubarb into the kitchen in the late 18th century. Before then, it was seen as purely medicinal. I'm fond of it stewed with a little ginger and a crumble topping. I would go so far as to say that any Englishman saying 'no' to rhubarb crumble should have his citizenship revoked.

CHICORY I have included chicory in the salads list because that's how I see it, although it's really a vegetable. I love the stubby little things – white, crisp leaves infused with yellow – and nothing can compare with that bitter chicory flavour.

Chicory is also very handy. That elongated spear-shaped leaf that curls upward and inward at the sides makes it an excellent carrying vessel for other foodstuffs, particularly seafood.

As a salad leaf they look delicate enough, and kept whole the heads braise well in stock. This takes away most of the bitterness and softens them.

As well as the traditional white and yellow, a vivid red variety is now available, although for some maddening reason the heads seem to be half the size of their white and yellow brothers.

COS This is a long, rounded, light green salad head with a very mild flavour and perhaps a slight taste of nuttiness. Also known as Romaine, it has been made famous as the main ingredient in a Caesar salad.

Controversy surrounds its name. A few textbooks will tell you it must have originated from the Greek island of Cos. Others say *cos* is the Arabic word for 'lettuce'. If I was a gambling man I'd back the second theory, if only because the cos lettuce is eaten all over the Arab world; it's one of the only salad heads that will stand up to extreme heat.

CUCUMBER The cucumber is a member of the cucurbit family, which makes it a close relation to the marrow and courgette (obviously!), and the melon. This latter may seem surprising, but their innards are amazingly similar and they both have a very high water content. In fact, your average cucumber is 96 per cent water.

Nearly all cucumbers these days are smooth of skin. Originally, the smooth ones were a delicacy grown expensively under heated glass, and the more common varieties had thicker skins that were ridged. The latter – known as ridge cucumbers – are rare today and very nice they are too (my girlfriend's grandfather used to grow them). A gherkin is a dwarf variety of cucumber.

Cucumbers used to be quite bitter and our grandmothers had to salt then wash them to remove the bitterness. That bitterness has been bred out of them now, but salting will still reduce the water content of your cucumber and intensify the flavour.

If you're going to cut your cucumber into chunks I recommend removing the skin. It's not a nice texture and its taste is slightly bitter. If you're going to slice your cucumber thinly then leave the skins on.

DANDELION Popular in France, legend had it that dandelion could make you wet yourself. This is why, years ago, it was known as 'wet the bed' or, in France, as *pissenlit*. I love dandelion – and I've never had any trouble! The name 'dandelion' is a corruption of *dent de lion*, meaning 'lion's tooth', because of its long serrated leaves.

Dandelion has a round, circular base, with many long yellow tendrils sprouting from it. A word of warning; it's very bitter. In its wild state it's nearly always green, but don't bother picking the green, it's disgusting. Most of the commercial varieties available to us have been blanched and are yellow.

I enjoy the bitter taste of raw dandelion leaves, especially when drizzled with a honey dressing. They can also be cooked gently like spinach, which reduces the bitterness.

FRISÉE Many people refer to this as curly endive. In a frisée the heart is the most important thing. You only want the pale yellow/white middle of the lettuce. The outside green leaves are sharp and bitter and virtually inedible.

Frisées are tough to grow, because of blanching the middle to get that sweet heart. Horticulturally, blanching means depriving the whole or part of the plant of sunlight. Blanching the middle of a frisée means covering the middle of the plant. As the plant gets bigger, and the middle gets bigger, the thing you're covering it with has to get bigger as well. You can imagine the trouble involved, I'm sure.

During the warmer months, frisées are slim and fine. As it gets colder, they get bigger and coarser. Don't bother with them then. Even though the frisée heart is milder than the green surround, it still holds on to a slight chicory bitterness. This means it contrasts beautifully with a sweeter salad dressing.

GEM/LITTLE GEM These are like miniature dumpy, pale green cos lettuces. I prefer them to cos as they're easier to wash and prepare and have a sweeter and crunchier heart. They also stand up to cooking. French peas is one of my favourite dishes: combine gem lettuces and peas in a saucepan with crème fraîche. The little green beauties soften up and absorb all the other flavours in the pan.

LOLLO ROSSO (*see* page 76)

OAKLEAF (*see* page 76)

ROCKET (*see* page 76 and recipes, pages 98–101)

SPRING ONION Who doesn't enjoy a spring onion and how does a little thing like that pack so much heat? Chopped and tossed in a salad they're wonderful, but they also work brilliantly when used to dip in sauces, like a natural tasting spoon.

Spring onions are available most of the year. They were originally an immature onion that started to sprout up in spring. Nowadays varieties have been developed with more and more white and less and less green. Spring onions now come in lots of sizes, from thinner than a pencil, to bigger than a leek. Generally the thinner they are, the milder they are.

WATERCRESS (*see* page 120)

HERBS

CHERVIL Chervil is the most delicate of herbs, not just in its flavour, which is a mix of parsley and tarragon, but also in appearance, almost like fine lace. It's also the first herb to turn when cut. Being so mild, it is best used with other mild flavours such as eggs or fish. If you are going to use chervil in a salad, use a lot, or it will just disappear, from sight as well as in flavour.

CORIANDER You can tell where you are in the world by people's use of herbs. If you see parsley everywhere, you are in the western hemisphere; if coriander is everywhere, you've entered the eastern half. Coriander looks like a smaller flat-leaf parsley; in fact the French call coriander 'Arab parsley'.

I'm not a huge fan. I can take it when it's cooked but in its raw state it smells like the little puddles my cat Fester used to leave. The upper leaves on a bunch are always smaller and much lighter in taste.

Coriander is used to flavour stews and curries. Always mash up the stem as well, as do South-East Asian people. Chefs cooking Thai food over here always ask for bunches with the roots intact, which makes the herb much more expensive; if you pull the whole root out, you won't get another cutting. The seeds are also widely used in Eastern cuisine.

DILL Mostly seen in the UK with fish, dill is more widely used in Scandinavia and Eastern Europe. A member of the parsley family, it has a slight aniseed flavour, which goes well with fish, boiled potatoes, beetroot, eggs and soured cream. It is a delicate herb and should be added at the end of cooking. In Greece it is paired with broad beans and artichokes.

MINT (*see* page 121)

PARSLEY Without a doubt this is the most popular herb in European cookery, used for both flavour and decoration.

There is fierce debate over the benefits of flat-leaf over curly-leaved varieties, and vice versa. Most modern cooks tell you that the flat-leaf is superior in flavour to the curly, which is rubbish. What alters the flavour of this herb is the length of time between pulling it from the ground and using it. A fresh sprig of parsley has much more flavour, whether its leaves are curly or flat. The one advantage flat has over curly is that you can chop it very finely. Curly can't be chopped well at all, it just turns into green mulch.

My favourite way with it is added to a white sauce to be served with bacon. Becky, one of the finalists on *MasterChef*, served venison steaks with a large amount of parsley on top, which was very good. Try to use the stalks as well as the leaves, as there is far more concentrated flavour in the stalks.

ROSEMARY (*see* page 121)

SAGE (*see* page 121)

THYME (*see* page 121)

Lamb

(*see also* page 16) This is definitely my favourite meat. There's lots of fat on lamb, which keeps it moist when cooking, meaning it can stand longer cooking than most meat. The perfect colour on cooked meat is a matter of personal choice and can bring about fierce debate. Personally, I think far too many chefs undercook lamb. Nervous of being accused of overcooking, they err far too dramatically on the side of caution. I serve mine with a hint of pink.

Because of the fat, lamb can take strong flavours. Garlic, thyme, rosemary and mint are perfect accompaniments. A plea: please serve with mint sauce. A little fresh mint chopped up with some white wine vinegar is the perfect sharp and sweet accompaniment for this fatty meat. In Italy, a country whose cuisine I much admire, they place anchovies over the joint before roasting it. The anchovies dissolve completely, leaving their salt, which emphasizes the flavour of the lamb.

Lamb stew

This does take a long time to cook, as all stews should, but the results are well worth it!

30g (1¼ oz) butter
2 tbsp vegetable oil
1kg (2¼ lb) best end of neck of lamb, in single ribs
5 tbsp seasoned plain flour
2 onions, peeled and chopped
500g (18oz) young carrots, washed and thinly sliced
500ml (18fl oz) lamb or chicken stock, hot

1 tbsp tomato purée
1 bouquet garni
salt and pepper
8 button onions or small shallots, peeled
8 new potatoes, scrubbed and halved

Serves 4

Preheat the oven to 170°C/325°F/Gas 3. Heat a large frying pan over a medium heat, and melt the butter and oil. Coat the lamb in 3 tbsp seasoned flour and brown all over in the fat. Remove from the pan and put in a casserole. Add the chopped onion and sliced carrot to the casserole.

Stir 2 tbsp of the seasoned flour into the used frying pan and cook over a low heat for 2 minutes. Gradually add the hot stock, whisking. Add the tomato purée and bring the sauce to the boil.

Pour the sauce over the meat and vegetables in the casserole. Add the bouquet garni and some seasoning. Cover the casserole and place in the oven for 1½ hours.

After this time, put the peeled onions or shallots and the potatoes on top of the casserole, and put back in the oven for about an hour, until the potatoes are cooked.

Remove the bouquet garni before serving.

Herb-stuffed shoulder of lamb

If you say 'no' to a shoulder of lamb you might as well say 'no' to life. Succulent meat infused with all those herbs is one of my favourite things to eat. Do two shoulders and have the second one for lunches throughout the week.

1 shoulder of lamb, boned
salt and pepper
2 tbsp chopped chives
4 tbsp chopped parsley leaves
2 tbsp chopped oregano
1 tbsp chopped rosemary
1 tbsp grated fresh root ginger

3 tbsp olive oil

GRAVY
125ml (4fl oz) red wine
125ml (4fl oz) lamb or chicken stock
1 tbsp cornflour

Serves 4–6

Preheat the oven to 180°C/350°F/Gas 4. Open up the boned meat so it lies flat, skin-side down. Cover with clingfilm and pound with a meat mallet or rolling pin until the meat is more or less the same thickness throughout.

Season the meat evenly with salt and pepper. Mix the chopped herbs and ginger with the oil. Spread this herb mixture over the meat (keep away from the edges). Now roll the meat up like a Swiss roll, doing this quite tightly. Tie the rolled-up joint at 5cm (2in) intervals with kitchen string. Brush the joint with a little extra oil. Season all over.

Now heat a large frying pan and fry the joint until brown, then place in a roasting tin and cook for 1–1½ hours, depending on how large the joint is (allow 20 minutes per 450g/1lb for meat that is pink in the centre, 25 minutes if you prefer it well done). When done, transfer to a plate. Cover with foil and set aside for 20 minutes.

Skim off any fat from the roasting tin. Place the tin over a medium heat and add the red wine and stock. Scrape the crusty bits from the tin, and cook to let the liquid reduce a little. Mix the cornflour with a little water and pour this mixture into the gravy. Cook over a low heat for a couple of minutes. Check the seasoning. Cut the roasted joint into thick slices and serve with the gravy.

Lamb steaks with honey and mustard glaze

The combination of mustard and honey, once cooked, gives a tangy sweetness to this very meaty chunk. This works wonderfully on the barbecue.

4 tbsp runny honey
4 tbsp mild mustard
salt and pepper
4 lamb steaks

Serves 4

Mix together the honey, mustard, salt and pepper. Spread half over the steaks. Now grill under a moderate heat, quite close to the heat, for about 6 minutes or so.

Turn the steaks over and use the rest of the glaze to coat. Place under the grill again for about 5–6 minutes. The cooking time will depend on the size of the steaks. Try to keep them a little pink inside.

Veal

(*see also* page 15) No one can condone the treatment traditionally associated with the young calves that make veal. They were kept in crates and not allowed to move around just so the meat would stay white. Many people in the world still believe the whiter veal to be superior and turn their noses up at anything with a hint of pink. I disagree. Redder or rose veal is very flavoursome meat. At least with pink-tinged meat you know the calf has led a more natural existence.

Veal is a firm, tender and creamy meat. It has very little fat and no marbling. Actually it does have fat running through it but it's so fine it's virtually impossible to see. There is no denying it, veal is expensive and a luxury.

Osso buco

Yeah, I know Osso Buco is Italian, but I cook a very good one and I thought I'd share it with you. It is traditionally served with risotto milanese, which is a simple saffron-flavoured risotto.

6 pieces shin of rose veal, about 4cm (1½ in) thick
a little seasoned plain flour
55g (2oz) butter
2 tbsp olive oil
3 carrots, peeled and finely chopped
3 celery stalks, finely chopped
3 garlic cloves, peeled and crushed
250ml (9fl oz) white wine
250ml (9fl oz) veal or chicken stock
2 x 400g cans chopped plum tomatoes with juice

salt and pepper
1 tsp caster sugar
2 sprigs rosemary

GARNISH
4 tbsp finely chopped parsley
finely grated zest of 2 unwaxed lemons
3 garlic cloves, peeled and finely chopped

Serves 6

Coat the veal with seasoned flour. Melt the butter and olive oil in a large pan. When the butter stops sizzling, add the meat and brown on both sides for a few minutes. Remove the meat from the pan and set aside.

Now add the chopped vegetables and garlic to the pan. Fry over a medium heat for a few minutes, allowing them to get some colour. Return the veal to the pan, and pour over the wine, stock and tomatoes. Season well with salt and pepper, and add the sugar and rosemary. Simmer, covered, for about 1½ hours, or until the meat is tender.

In the meantime, mix together the garnish ingredients.

When the meat is cooked, if the sauce is too liquid, remove the lid, raise the heat and simmer until really thick. It is easier if you remove the meat and keep it warm while you do this.

Serve with the garnish sprinkled over the top.

Veal parcels

This is perhaps my favourite dish of all time! It's fun to prepare, it's beautiful, and it tastes divine.

6 x 2cm (¾ in) slices shoulder of rose veal/
  veal escalope
200g (7oz) smoked bacon rashers
175g (6oz) sliced ham
4 medium eggs, beaten
3 tbsp crème fraîche

salt and pepper
55g (2oz) butter
100g (3½oz) dill pickles, finely chopped
1 tbsp plain flour
350ml (12fl oz) chicken stock

Serves 6

Preheat the oven to 180°C/350°F/Gas 4. Place each slice of veal between pieces of clingfilm and beat with a rolling pin or meat mallet until evenly very thin. Cover each veal slice with a layer of bacon and ham.

Beat the eggs and crème fraîche together with a little seasoning. Melt 10g (¼oz) of the butter in a small pan over a medium heat. Add the egg mixture and cook until lightly scrambled, stirring all the time. Put a layer of egg over each slice of meat, spreading almost to the edges. Sprinkle with chopped dill pickles and season with pepper. Now roll up each slice of meat and tie the parcels securely with kitchen string.

In an ovenproof casserole, melt the remaining butter over a medium heat. Brown the parcels all over and season with pepper. Remove from the pan. Sprinkle the flour into the pan and cook for a couple of minutes. Slowly add half the stock, stirring constantly. Add the browned veal parcels and bring to the boil. Place the casserole in the oven (do not cover) and bake for about 2 hours, turning the rolls over after an hour. Keep checking that the liquid does not dry out. Use the remaining stock if necessary. When cooked, leave to sit for about 10 minutes before cutting off the string. Serve the parcels sliced into rings, with the gravy poured over.

Veal with port and mushroom sauce

You know you've cooked a good dish when your guests are scraping up every last bit of their sauce.

2 large knobs butter
1 tbsp vegetable oil
4 large, thin rose veal escalopes
salt and pepper
2 tbsp lemon juice
125g (4½oz) chestnut mushrooms, sliced

2 heaped tbsp finely chopped shallot
4 tbsp port
125ml (4fl oz) white wine
2 tbsp crème fraîche

Serves 4

Melt half the butter with the oil in a frying pan over a medium heat. When the butter stops sizzling, add the seasoned veal escalopes. Cook for 30 seconds on each side. Remove from the pan and set aside. Keep the pan to hand.

Heat the remaining butter with the juice in a separate pan. Add the mushrooms and cook for 5 minutes. Remove from the heat. Add the shallot to the veal frying pan and sweat for 2 minutes, then stir in the port and wine. Increase the heat, bring to the boil and reduce the liquid by half. Add the mushrooms and crème fraîche. Stir over a low heat. Check the seasoning, then add the cooked veal and simmer until heated through.

Monkfish

(*see also* page 24) Monkfish flesh is dense, meaty, white and lean. It is virtually boneless and the cooked flesh comes away from the spine easily. The quality of the fish and the lack of small bones has made it very popular and therefore very expensive. You should always skin the fish before cooking, but also be aware of the membrane that lies just under the skin. This should also be removed or it will shrink in the heat around that delicate flesh. The monkfish may be meaty, but it has a high water content. Cook it with as little liquid as you can, if any at all. The denseness of the flesh makes it perfect for roasting or grilling.

Monkfish kebabs

Here's one for the barbecue if you get a warm spring day – although personally I would prefer to eat the kebabs indoors and then lie out in the garden afterwards!

500g (18oz) monkfish fillet, skinned
4 tbsp olive oil
juice and finely grated zest of 1 lemon
2 tbsp finely chopped dill
salt and pepper

Serves 4

Cut the fish into 2.5cm (1in) cubes and place in a bowl. Whisk the oil, lemon juice and zest, dill, salt and pepper together. Pour over the fish and leave to marinate for about 4 hours.

Peel the cucumber, and cut in half lengthwise. Using a teaspoon, scoop out the seeds. Cut the shell into 2cm (¾in) slices. Melt the butter in a small pan, add the cucumber slices and cook gently for about 2 minutes, until beginning to soften. Set aside.

Preheat the grill to its highest setting.

Drain the fish, keeping the marinade. Thread the cubes of fish with slices of cucumber on to small skewers or bamboo sticks. Two sticks per person looks nice.

Brush the kebabs with marinade and grill for about 5 minutes on each side.

Spring monkfish stew

Wow! I absolutely love this: big chunks of meaty fish and the best of the spring vegetables. The chervil, which I consider to be a much undervalued herb, adds the lightest of touches and makes the dish complete.

200g (7oz) podded broad beans
30g (1¼ oz) butter
3 tbsp vegetable oil
1 onion, peeled and thinly sliced
250g (9oz) baby carrots, scrubbed
1 garlic clove, peeled and crushed
225g (8oz) asparagus, trimmed, each stalk cut into 3
750g (1lb 10oz) monkfish fillet, skinned and cut into large chunks

a little seasoned plain flour
150ml (5fl oz) white wine
300ml (10fl oz) fish stock
1 tbsp lemon juice
3 tbsp crème fraîche
3 tbsp chopped chervil
salt and pepper

Serves 4

Drop the broad beans into unsalted boiling water and cook for 3 minutes. Drain and cool under running water. Slip them out of their skins. Set aside.

Heat half the butter and half the oil in a large pan over a medium heat. Add the onion, carrots, garlic and asparagus, and sweat until just starting to brown. Remove from the pan and set aside. Keep the pan to hand.

Dip the fish into the flour, shaking well to remove excess. Melt the remaining butter and oil in a clean frying pan over a medium heat. Add the fish and brown all over, a few minutes. Remove from the pan and set aside.

Add the wine to the vegetable pan, scraping up the residue. When boiling, add the carrot mixture and fish, and pour over the stock. Bring to the boil, reduce to a simmer and cook with a lid on for 8 minutes, or until the fish is cooked. Stir in the beans, lemon juice, crème fraîche and chervil, and heat through. Season to taste before serving.

Baked monkfish

This is a lovely, natural way of cooking. All of these flavours blending together are great.

1 piece of monkfish fillet, about 175–200g
   (6–7oz), skinned
salt and pepper
1 tsp lemon juice

2 tbsp crème fraîche
1 tbsp finely chopped dill

Serves 1

Preheat the oven to 220°C/425°F/Gas 7. Lay a large piece of foil on the work surface for the piece of fish.

Put the fish on the foil, and season. Top with the lemon juice, a dollop of crème fraîche, then the dill.

Wrap up the parcel so that there are no leaks, but leaving some air inside so the fish can steam.

Bake for about 20–25 minutes, depending on the thickness of the fish. If cooking more than one parcel, try not to place them too close together or the cooking time will have to be increased. When cooked, open the parcel. Drain the juices into a bowl, whisk up and serve poured over the fish.

(*see also* page 25) Absolutely superb little things, these sweet, clean little muscles have a unique flavour that should be savoured. The scallop is the most beautiful edible mollusc. Everything about it is stylish and elegant, even the way it moves; the muscle inside is used to open the shell and this propels it through the water.

Scallop chowder

You may think pork and scallops is an odd combination: I promise you it isn't. This dish is big and hearty and I think the textures and flavours will surprise you.

1.5kg (3lb) belly pork in one piece
1 knob butter
1 large onion, peeled and finely sliced
4 medium potatoes, peeled and diced
1 carrot, peeled and diced
1 parsnip, peeled and diced
1 green pepper, seeded and sliced
2 celery stalks, roughly chopped

600ml (1 pint) full-fat milk
salt and pepper
juice of 1 orange
12 scallops, cleaned, with corals
juice of 1 lemon
300ml (10 fl oz) fish stock

Serves 4–6

Place a large sauté pan over a medium heat. When hot, add the piece of belly pork, skin-side down, and cook until brown and the fat is running. Remove the pork and set aside.

Melt the butter in the pan. Add the onion and cook for about 5 minutes without browning. Now add the potato, carrot, parsnip, green pepper and celery, and sweat for about 10 minutes with the lid on. Do not brown.

Add the milk and bring to a simmer. Season with salt and pepper, and add the orange juice and pork. Simmer the chowder, covered, until the vegetables are cooked, about 20–25 minutes.

Meanwhile, wash the scallops in cold water. Cover with lemon juice and allow to stand for 15 minutes. Cut each scallop in half, leaving the corals whole. Place the scallops in a pan with the fish stock. Bring to the boil, reduce the heat and simmer for 5 minutes.

Lift the pork out of the soup pan – it should be cooked through – and discard the skin and fat. Dice the flesh, and return it to the chowder along with the scallops and fish stock. Heat up, check the seasoning, and serve.

Scallops with garlic butter sauce

I can still remember my first scallop, at the Blueprint Café in London. After all these years, I still can't resist them. This sauce is easy and very sympathetic to the scallop.

500g (18oz) scallops, shelled and trimmed
a little seasoned plain flour
75g (2½oz) butter
1 tbsp olive oil
2 garlic cloves, peeled and finely chopped

2 tbsp chopped parsley leaves
salt and pepper
lemon wedges, to serve

Serves 4

Cover the scallops lightly with seasoned flour, shaking to remove any excess. Melt 15g (½oz) of the butter with the oil in a frying pan. When the foam subsides, fry the scallops gently over a medium heat for about 1½ minutes on each side, until lightly browned. Transfer to a heated dish and keep warm.

Put the remaining butter in a small jug and melt in a microwave. Pour the melted butter into a clean frying pan, discarding the milky solids at the bottom of the jug. Place the pan over a medium heat until the butter sizzles. Stir in the garlic and heat for about a minute. Remove from the heat, and stir in the parsley and some seasoning. Add the scallops for 10 seconds to warm through.

Serve garnished with lemon wedges.

Scallop and bacon kebabs

You can make these kebabs without the sauce, but I think the sauce is very good. The difference the butter makes to the reduction is incredible.

750g (1lb 10oz) scallops, shelled and trimmed
125ml (4fl oz) white wine
1 tbsp light soy sauce
1 tbsp olive oil
250g (9oz) unsmoked streaky bacon

55g (2oz) butter, cold and cubed
salt and pepper

Serves 6

Put the scallops in a small bowl, and cover with the white wine, soy sauce and olive oil. Leave for 20 minutes to marinate. Drain, keeping the marinade.

Heat the grill as hot as possible. Using a heavy knife against a chopping board, stretch each bacon rasher, then cut each strip in half. Roll each scallop in a bacon piece and thread on to skewers (but not too tightly).

Grill the kebabs, turning frequently, for about 6–7 minutes, until the scallops are just cooked.

Meanwhile, put the marinade into a small pan and bring to the boil. Reduce the liquid by half. Whisk in the cubes of butter gradually.

Serve the butter sauce with the grilled kebabs.

Asparagus

(*see also* page 25) This vegetable has a very short season and is without doubt one of the highlights of the culinary year. I shouldn't worry too much about the size of your spears. There's nothing wrong with cutting the big jumbo ones in half if you have to. When you buy, look at two things: the heads and the stems. The heads should be tightly closed: as they age, they open up and try to flower. The stems should be smooth and wrinkle-free. The best indication of freshness is to feel the base of the spear. If the asparagus has just been cut, the bottom will be wet. It dries after cutting, soon turns hard, and then browns and becomes very rough indeed.

Many people are unsure where to cut their asparagus before cooking. Hold the spear between thumb and forefinger and wiggle it. Start in the middle and work your way down. When you get to the bit that won't wiggle, cut it off.

Asparagus with tarragon hollandaise

This is a real classic – and unbeatable!

400g (14oz) asparagus

HOLLANDAISE SAUCE
115g (4oz) unsalted butter
2 medium egg yolks

1 tbsp lemon juice
salt and white pepper
2 tsp finely chopped tarragon leaves

Serves 2

Snap off and discard the woody stems from the asparagus. Wash the remaining stalks well.

Bring a large pan of salted water to the boil. Melt the butter for the sauce gently in another small pan.

Add the asparagus to the boiling water and bring back to the boil. Reduce the heat, and simmer until the asparagus is just soft, about 5–10 minutes.

While the asparagus is cooking, put the egg yolks and lemon juice in a food processor and whizz for 30 seconds. Now add some white pepper, turn on the processor again, and add the melted butter in a very thin constant stream. Try to leave out the white bits of the butter, or you'll have a bitty sauce. Add some salt.

Pour the sauce into a clean bowl and stir in the tarragon. Taste as you go; tarragon is a powerful herb.

Transfer the asparagus to a plate and pour over the hollandaise sauce. Serve immediately.

Chilled asparagus soup

This is a very good way of using up tired or even misshapen late-season 'grass'. Enjoy it in your garden with a chilled glass of Chardonnay. Oh, bliss!

700g (1lb 9oz) asparagus
salt and pepper
30g (1¼ oz) butter
2 onions, peeled and thinly sliced

1.4 litres (2½ pints) vegetable stock
150ml (5fl oz) single cream

Serves 6

Wash the asparagus under cold water. Cut off the tips and simmer these gently in salted water until just tender, about 3–5 minutes. Drain carefully and put aside to cool.

Snap off and discard the woody part of the asparagus stalks. Now thinly slice the stalks. Melt the butter gently in a large saucepan, add the stalks and the onion, cover the pan and sweat gently for 10 minutes.

Add the stock and season very well. Bring to the boil and simmer, lid on, for 40 minutes.

Purée the soup in a food processor until smooth. Sieve this into a clean pan to remove any stringy bits. Stir in the cream and heat gently. Now check the seasoning again: chilled soup will need more seasoning than hot. Now stir in the asparagus tips.

Refrigerate for at least 3 hours until very cold. Serve into bowls, making sure everybody gets an equal amount of the asparagus tips.

Peas

(see also page 26) The pea is both sweet and soft. It is the most wonderful of vegetables, of that there is no doubt.

Minted pea soup

I do enjoy this, but then I love mint and peas. They are truly a marriage made in heaven.

55g (2oz) butter
1 onion, peeled and finely chopped
1kg (2¼ lb) fresh peas, podded (or 500g/18oz frozen)
1.2 litres (2 pints) vegetable or chicken stock
½ tsp caster sugar
3 large sprigs mint

salt and pepper
2 medium egg yolks
150ml (5fl oz) single cream or crème fraîche

Serves 6

Melt the butter in a large pan, add the onion and sweat for about 5 minutes, until soft but not coloured. Add the peas, stock, sugar, 2 sprigs of the mint and some seasoning. Bring to the boil, cover and simmer for 30 minutes.

Now either blitz the soup in a food processor, sieve it, or just use a stick blender to whizz it to the consistency you prefer. Return it to the pan, check the seasoning and place over a low heat.

In a bowl beat the egg yolks together with the cream or crème fraîche and add to the soup. Stir the cream mixture thoroughly into the soup. Do not boil or the soup will turn into thick, green, scrambled eggs.

Serve each bowl garnished with a couple of leaves of fresh mint.

Peas and fresh tuna

Please, please, you have to cook this, it's just so tasty. Meaty pieces of very good fish matched perfectly by peas – and it looks so good.

4 tbsp olive oil
1 onion, peeled and thinly sliced
1 garlic clove, peeled and crushed
4 tuna steaks, about 150–200g (5½–7oz) each
salt and pepper
5 tbsp white wine

2 tsp tomato purée
½ tsp caster sugar
250g (9oz) cooked peas
3 tsp chopped parsley leaves, to garnish

Serves 4

Heat the oil in a large frying pan over a medium heat. Fry the onion and garlic together for about 5 minutes, until slightly browned. Remove from the pan and set aside.

In the same pan, fry the seasoned tuna steaks on both sides until lightly browned, about 3 minutes.

Mix the wine, tomato purée and sugar together, and pour over the tuna along with the cooked onions and garlic. Cover the pan and cook over a very low heat for about 10 minutes.

Add the peas, season and heat through for a few minutes. Garnish with parsley, and serve.

Peas and shallots with cream

This is a lovely accompaniment for any meat. My preference is for a big lump of honeyed ham.

30g (1¼ oz) butter
175g (6oz) small shallots, peeled
350g (12oz) podded fresh peas (or frozen)
salt and pepper
150ml (5fl oz) crème fraîche

15g (½ oz) plain flour
2 tsp chopped parsley leaves
about 1 tsp lemon juice

Serves 4

Melt the butter in a large frying pan, add the shallots and fry gently for about 5 minutes over a medium heat until they are brown.

Add the peas, season and stir for a couple of minutes. Add 125ml (4fl oz) water and bring to the boil. Cover the pan and simmer for about 10 minutes, until the onions are cooked through. There should still be a thin layer of liquid on the base of the pan. If there is too much liquid, remove the lid and increase the heat until the liquid is reduced.

Mix the crème fraîche and flour together in a small bowl, using a small whisk. Stir this mixture into the peas along with the parsley. Cook over a low heat for 3–4 minutes, until the sauce is thick. Check the seasoning, adding lemon juice to sharpen the taste, then serve.

Sprouting broccoli

(*see also* page 27) The first sprouting broccoli to become popular was the purple variety. Green and white are just as good.

Sprouting broccoli tart

You can use any cheese for this tart. I picked Parmesan because it's got those little salt crusts in it.

PASTRY
250g (9oz) plain flour
a pinch of salt
125g (4½ oz) butter, cold and cubed
1-2 tbsp cold water
1 medium egg yolk, beaten

FILLING
700g (1lb 9oz) sprouting broccoli, trimmed

20g (¾ oz) butter
1 tbsp water
2 medium eggs
175g (6 oz) cream cheese
125ml (4fl oz) single cream
4 tbsp freshly grated Parmesan
salt and pepper

Serves 4–5

To make the pastry, put the flour, salt and butter in a food processor. Whizz until the mixture is like breadcrumbs. Add the cold water and whizz briefly until a dough forms. If the dough is too dry, add a further teaspoon of water. Knead on a floured surface quickly. Cover with clingfilm and chill in the refrigerator for 30 minutes.

Preheat the oven to 190°C/375°F/Gas 5. Roll out the pastry on a floured work surface and use to line a 23cm (9in) flan tin. Prick the base with a fork. Use scrunched-up foil to line the sides of the pastry and bake blind for 10 minutes. Remove from the oven, and brush inside the pastry case with the egg yolk. Return to the oven, and bake for a further 5 minutes.

Meanwhile, for the filling, chop the broccoli into small pieces that will fit the flan tin. Melt the butter in a pan over a medium heat. Add the broccoli and water, cover and cook for 4 minutes. Drain the broccoli and place in the pastry shell. Beat the eggs in a bowl, add the cream cheese and mix until smooth. Stir in the cream, Parmesan and seasoning. Pour over the broccoli and bake for 30 minutes.

Sprouting broccoli with almonds

For me, the combination of almonds and lemon juice is reminiscent of holidays in North Africa.

400g (14oz) sprouting broccoli, washed and trimmed
salt and pepper
90g (3¼ oz) butter

30g (1¼ oz) flaked almonds
1 tbsp lemon juice

Serves 4

Bring a pan of salted water to the boil. Drop in the broccoli, and cook for 3–4 minutes until tender. Drain.

Melt the butter in a large frying pan. When hot add the almonds and fry gently until golden brown. Add the lemon juice. Add the cooked broccoli to heat through.

Spring greens

(*see also* page 27) The colour of spring greens is not as strong as that of green cabbage, and neither is the flavour. This isn't a bad thing as not everybody enjoys the strong, earthy taste of cabbage, especially children. In fact, spring greens are a good introduction for infants into the world of cabbage. They lend themselves to lighter cooking and are pleasing shredded and eaten raw.

Spring green parcels

Dinner guests are always surprised by this one. I don't think anybody expects to find all that flavour inside a cabbage leaf, and the great taste of iron that the spring greens give makes me think that every mouthful must be good for me.

2 large heads spring greens
salt and pepper
1 tbsp vegetable oil
1 large knob butter
3 tbsp finely chopped shallot
4 rashers streaky bacon, rinded and finely chopped
250g (9oz) minced chicken

40g (1½ oz) Parmesan, freshly and finely grated
4 medium eggs, hard-boiled, shelled and chopped
55g (2oz) fresh white breadcrumbs
1 tbsp golden syrup
300ml (10fl oz) well-flavoured chicken stock

Serves 4

Preheat the oven to 180°C/350°F/Gas 4. Peel 8 large leaves off the greens and trim away the hard ribs. Blanch the leaves for about 3–4 minutes in a large pan of boiling salted water. You just want to soften the leaves so they can be rolled. Drain, refresh with cold water, and drain well again.

Finely chop 250g (9oz) of the heart from the greens. In a large frying pan, melt the oil and butter over a medium heat. Add the shallot, and sweat for a couple of minutes. Add the bacon and chopped greens, and sweat together for about 5 minutes. Set aside and leave to cool.

Mix the cooled shallot mixture with the chicken, Parmesan, eggs and breadcrumbs. Season with salt and pepper and mix well again.

Now stuff the cold leaves with the stuffing. Fold the sides of each leaf over the stuffing and roll up like a Swiss roll. Place folded-side down in a large ovenproof dish.

Mix the syrup with the stock and pour over the leaves. Cover the dish with foil, and bake for about an hour, until the stuffing is cooked through. The parcels should be browned and the juice quite reduced.

Spring greens with garlic

You could eat this as a side dish, but I think it's definitely good enough to be a starter.

1kg (2¼ lb) spring greens, washed
salt and pepper
2 tbsp olive oil

4 garlic cloves, peeled and finely chopped

Serves 4

Remove and discard the outside leaves and any tough stalks from the spring greens. Roll up a few leaves at a time and cut into fine strips.

Blanch the greens in boiling salted water for about 2 minutes. Drain and rinse under cold running water. Squeeze out any excess water.

Heat the olive oil in a wok over a medium heat. Add the garlic and cook for just a minute. Add the dried greens, season and toss to coat in the oil and garlic. Cook for 2–3 minutes until heated through.

Spring greens baked with cream

This tastes so good, I'm often tempted to serve it as a dish in its own right.

1 large knob butter
700g (1lb 9oz) spring greens, washed and shredded
55g (2oz) toasted hazelnuts, chopped
30g (1¼ oz) fresh white breadcrumbs
175ml (6fl oz) crème fraîche

1 tbsp caster sugar
1 tsp paprika
salt and pepper
55g (2oz) mature Cheddar, grated

Serves 4

Preheat the oven to 170°C/325°F/Gas 3. Place the butter in a large saucepan and add the shredded greens. Put the pan over a medium-high heat, cover and cook for about 4 minutes, shaking the pot now and again. The greens should be just cooked with a crunch.

Put the greens in a gratin dish. Mix the hazelnuts and breadcrumbs together. Separately, mix together the crème fraîche, sugar, paprika, seasoning and half the cheese and mix with the greens.

Sprinkle the remaining cheese over the top of the gratin dish, followed by the breadcrumb mixture. Bake for about 30 minutes, until golden and bubbling.

New and salad potatoes (*see also* page 26)

To tell new potatoes from salad potatoes do the skin test. The skin of the new potato flakes away. Do you know why? Because it's a new potato! I consider the Jersey Royal to be the *crème de la crème* of new potatoes.

Jersey and red onion salad

There's plenty of allium zing giving bite to this salad.

675g (1½lb) Jersey Royal potatoes, scrubbed
salt and pepper
3 tbsp olive oil
1 tbsp white wine vinegar
2 spring onions, thinly sliced

1 red onion, peeled and thinly sliced
175ml (6fl oz) mayonnaise
3 tbsp chopped chives

Serves 4–6

Cook the potatoes in boiling salted water for about 10–15 minutes, until tender.

Mix together the oil and vinegar.

Drain the potatoes thoroughly and place in a large bowl. Add the oil and vinegar mixture and the sliced onions. Season. Put the bowl aside to cool.

When the potato mixture is cool, add the mayonnaise and chives and mix thoroughly. Chill before serving.

Fried Jerseys with garlic mayonnaise

Pure self-indulgence, this one – Jersey potato chips!

500g (18oz) Jersey Royal potatoes, scrubbed
vegetable oil, for shallow-frying

GARLIC MAYONNAISE

1 large egg yolk
½ tsp Dijon mustard

salt and pepper
250ml (9fl oz) mild olive oil
2 garlic cloves, peeled and crushed
1–2 tbsp lemon juice

Serves 4

To make the garlic mayonnaise, put the egg yolk in a small bowl with the mustard and a pinch of salt. Using a small whisk, beat in the olive oil. Do this very slowly, drop by drop at first, then in a thin stream as you get going. Add the crushed garlic and lemon juice to taste

Cook the potatoes in boiling salted water for 5 minutes. Turn off the heat, cover the pan, and leave to sit for 15 minutes. Drain thoroughly, using kitchen paper to dry the potatoes. Halve them if they are large.

Heat 2cm (¾in) vegetable oil in a large frying pan. When the oil is very hot, add the potatoes (carefully!) and fry quickly, turning often, until crisp and golden. It may be easier to do this in batches.

Drain the potatoes on kitchen paper, season with salt and pepper and serve with the garlic mayonnaise.

Minted Jerseys

This is the way to infuse the flavour of mint into this most celebrated of spuds.

1kg (2¼lb) Jersey Royal potatoes, scrubbed
salt and pepper
55g (2oz) butter, broken into bits
10g (¼oz) fresh mint leaves, finely chopped

Serves 6

Preheat the oven to 190°C/375°F/Gas 5. Place the potatoes on a large piece of tin foil. Season and add the butter and mint. Enclose the potatoes in a loose parcel, sealing the edges well. Leave quite a lot of room in the parcel so the spuds can steam.

Place the foil packet on a baking sheet and bake for about 40 minutes. Check that the potatoes are cooked thoroughly before serving.

Rhubarb

(*see also* page 27) Rhubarb is very sour in its natural state and it takes an alarmingly large amount of sweetening. It does have other uses apart from in a pudding. I was once served it very successfully with a slice of foie gras. Its sweet-sour mixture also makes it a perfect accompaniment for game birds. One word of warning: don't attempt to eat the leaves as they are highly acidic and poisonous.

A special mention should go to 'champagne' rhubarb. Yorkshire was once famed for it. It is forced in hot-houses and the resulting stem is thin and pink. Over the years, I have seen this develop into a real luxury item, akin to asparagus.

Rhubarb, orange and ginger jam

The orange highlights the rhubarb in this jam, and the ginger takes it to a completely new level. I like to think of this as a cross between jam and marmalade; what you might call 'jamalade'!

9 oranges
7 lemons
1.5kg (3lb 5oz) rhubarb, trimmed and cut into 2cm (¾in) lengths
50g (2oz) fresh root ginger, peeled and finely chopped

1.2 litres (2 pints) water
2.5kg (5½lb) preserving sugar
5 pieces preserved ginger, finely chopped

Makes approx. 3kg (6½lb)

Preheat the oven to its lowest setting. Wash jam jars in hot, soapy water, rinse and place upside-down on a baking tray, using a clean tea-towel underneath to cushion them. Place the jars in the oven until ready to use.

Peel the orange zest off with a potato peeler and shred it finely. Squeeze the juice from the oranges and lemons.

Put two-thirds of the rhubarb in a preserving pan with the ginger, orange juice and zest, lemon juice and water.

Cut up the lemon shells, and remove and roughly chop the pith. Tie the pith and all the orange and lemon pips securely in a large piece of muslin. Add this to the pan.

Bring the mixture to the boil, reduce the heat and simmer for 1 hour, or until the volume has reduced by half.

Fish out the muslin bag and leave it to cool. Give it a squeeze, returning the juices to the pan. Discard the bag. Add the rest of the rhubarb to the pan, return to the boil and simmer for 10 minutes, until soft. Gradually stir in the sugar, stirring all the time until it is fully dissolved.

Bring the jam to the boil again and boil hard to setting point, 15–20 minutes. On a thermometer this is 105°C/221°F. Alternatively, put a saucer in the freezer in advance and, when you think the jam is ready, take the pan off the heat and put a teaspoon of jam on the cold saucer. When the jam is cool, run a finger through it. If it wrinkles, it is ready.

Now stir in the preserved ginger. Pot the jam into the warm jars. Cover each with a disc of waxed paper. When cool, cover with cellophane covers and lids. Store for up to a year.

Rhubarb meringue pie

OK, this dish does take a bit of work, but it is a chance to showcase your talents, and the results are spectacular.

PASTRY

200g (7oz) plain flour
25g (1oz) ground almonds
115g (4oz) butter, cold and cubed
1 medium egg yolk
1 tbsp water
2 tbsp caster sugar

FILLING

700g (1lb 9oz) rhubarb, washed and cut into 2cm
(¾in) pieces
250g (9oz) caster sugar
juice and finely grated zest of 3 oranges
3 medium eggs, separated
5 tbsp cornflour
4 tbsp water

Serves 6

Preheat the oven to 190°C/375°F/Gas 5. For the pastry, place the flour and almonds in a food processor. Add the butter and whizz until the mixture looks like breadcrumbs. Beat the egg yolk with the water and sugar and add this. Whizz to a dough. Turn on to a floured surface and knead briefly. Cover with clingfilm and chill for 30 minutes.

For the filling, put the rhubarb, 6 tbsp of the sugar and the orange juice and zest into a pan. Cover and cook gently until the fruit is just cooked. Follow the instructions for preparing and baking the pastry case on page 54, but this time using a fluted flan tin and baking initially for 15 minutes, then brushing the inside of the pastry casing with a little of the egg yolk for the filling, then baking for a further 15 minutes, until crisp.

Blend the cornflour and water in a bowl. Stir into the rhubarb, bring to the boil, and stir until thick. Take off the heat and quickly stir in the remaining egg yolk. Pour into the pastry case. Whisk the egg whites in a large bowl until they form stiff peaks. Gradually add the remaining sugar, a tablespoon at a time, whisking between each addition. Spoon the meringue in swirls over the fruit to cover. Bake for about 30 minutes, until the meringue is golden brown.

Rhubarb fool

This is soft, sweet and creamy. Twirl the fruit through the cream, or mush it all up together; the taste is the same.

500g (18oz) rhubarb
85g (3oz) caster sugar
300ml (10fl oz) double cream

250ml (9fl oz) crème fraîche

Serves 4

Preheat the oven to 200°C/400°F/Gas 6. Wash the fruit, trim the ends and cut the stems into 2.5cm (1in) lengths. Put the fruit in a large enough shallow baking dish to allow it to be in a single layer. Sprinkle over the sugar evenly.

Cover with foil and bake for 20 minutes. Remove the foil and shake the dish. The sugar should have dissolved. If not, return to the oven for another 5 minutes. The rhubarb pieces should be whole but cooked through. Leave to cool.

Beat the double cream to soft peaks, mix in the crème fraîche, then mix in the fruit and sweet juices, reserving some of the latter to pour over the top. Do not over-mix. Pour into small bowls and serve.

Summer

Summer ingredients

FISH

BREAM I'm not a fan of bream. It's full of bones and it lies in muddy water, which doesn't do anything for its flavour. To make matters worse, the bream you buy has normally been soaked, and that won't help the flavour either. It's up to you, give it a go if you want, but don't say I didn't warn you.

BRILL (*see* page 116)

COLEY (*see* page 24)

CRAB (*see* recipes, pages 82–85) Preparing a crab can be hard work. I remember in the last *Celebrity MasterChef* when, in one quarter-final, John and I left the celebrities with a whole crab and the most basic of instructions on how to dress one, with hilarious results. We had smashed shells, bleeding fingers, accidentally thrown-away claws, and in one case somebody threw all the brown meat away! If you are going to buy a ready-prepared crab, look at it closely and move it about a bit. If there is any liquid running out of it, it is old. Smell it too, because as it ages, it gives off the unmistakable pong of ammonia. Contrary to popular belief, the lungs, or wonderfully named 'dead man's fingers', are not poisonous. Disgusting, yes; poisonous, no.

Many connoisseurs claim the female crab is sweeter than the male. I don't know about that. What I can say is that the males are nearly always bigger and have more flesh. If you want to know the sex of a crab, look at its tail: females have broad tails; the male tail is narrower and comes to a point. The crab should be alive, kicking like mad when you move it. It's best to look for a big old hard shell. This means the shell has been on the crab for a while and the crab inside has filled into it. One last thing: you only get white meat from the claws and you only get brown from inside the shell.

DOVER SOLE Despite its name, it doesn't come from Dover, but most specimens of this lovely fish traditionally entered London via the Dover ports. It is a luxury fish, and the inflated price reflects this. It is a large flat fish with firm, white, superb, delicately flavoured flesh. Give it the respect it deserves and only cook it in the simplest of ways.

Nearly all fish should be absolutely spankingly fresh. Not so the Dover sole. To be at its best, the Dover needs to mature slightly – preferably for two to three days.

GREY MULLET (*see* page 116)

GURNARD The gurnard is cheap to buy with good reason, as its flesh is dry and full of bones. However, it's perfect for stews, soups and pies. It comes in a number of colours, but we mostly see the pretty red ones. The prettiness, unfortunately for the gurnard, ends there, as it's one of the most comical looking fish I've ever seen. It has a sloping armoured head ending in a mouth that looks like a duck's bill.

JOHN DORY (*see* page 24)

LANGOUSTINE (*see* page 24)

LEMON SOLE This fish actually belongs to the 'dab' family. It is flat though, and does look rather like a Dover sole. Although its flesh is not so good, it is still a marvellous fish. I think it suffers in the popularity stakes because it bears the name 'sole', and isn't quite as good as the Dover. It's a fine fish with a slightly salty flavour and, like the Dover, its skin comes away easily from the bone.

LOBSTER (*see* page 24)

MACKEREL The mackerel is a popular fish and tonnes are caught yearly. One reason for such a successful catch is that mackerel migrate in huge shoals back to the same breeding ground every year.

A fresh mackerel will shine and is easily identified by its blue-black stripy back; it's the only fish I can think of that is black inside its mouth. The French name, *maquereau*, is also the French for 'pimp'. I imagine this may be because the mackerel is such a flashy, shiny-looking creature.

The best way to cook mackerel is to grill it. It's very oily, and will fill your kitchen with smoke. It benefits from a sharp sauce to counterbalance the oil.

PLAICE (*see* page 25)

POLLACK
No, it's not 'pollock', it's 'pollack'. It is a member of the cod family and with the arguments over dwindling cod reserves, many say the pollack is a decent substitute. I'm not completely convinced. It's a decent enough fish, but it hasn't got quite the same flavour as cod. It doesn't look as attractive either. It's smaller, with a green-brown body.

PRAWNS (*see* page 117 and recipes, pages 138–141)

SALMON
I've heard many a heated debate on the subject of salmon farming. What I would say is that, because there's so much farmed salmon that is not fantastic, I've got bored with the fish. It's too simple to say all farmed salmon is bad. There are so many different salmon farms, all using many different techniques. Some are very good, some not good at all. But I've never eaten a farmed salmon that comes anywhere near the taste and texture of a wild one. Farmed fish is always rounder and fatter than the lean, hard, muscled wild fish.

The wild fish feeds on crustaceans, which is why its flesh is that beautiful pink colour. It feeds in salt water and then swims back into fresh water to spawn. As the fish makes this epic journey, it loses the body weight that it has built up while feeding in the sea. The best place to catch a wild salmon is at the mouth of the river, at the start of its journey, while it is still somewhere near full weight.

SEA BASS (*see* recipes, pages 78–81)
This is a beautiful looking beast. It is a dark steely grey with a white underbelly, similar to a salmon in appearance. When fresh, it's hard to the touch. It takes a bit of work, but your efforts will be well rewarded. The scales need scraping off, but before you do this, take a pair of sharp scissors to the fins;

all of them, not just the big ones on top, and be careful; even a dead sea bass can still wound.

Among fisherman, legend has it that the sea bass is the cleverest of fish and knows when someone is trying to catch it. It is undoubtedly true that the catch is always lower when the sun is shining and the water is clear. The catch is much higher with an overcast sky.

SEA TROUT
This fish is as near to a salmon as it can get without actually being one. It looks like a salmon, and even tastes like one. In fact, it's often called a salmon trout. If you are lucky enough to get one – but I doubt it; you hardly ever see them even in the best-stocked fishmongers – treat it in exactly the same way as you would a salmon.

SHRIMP
Any pink shrimp are imported foreigners. Our local shrimp are always brown and they are the smallest in the crustacean family. Their shells, even when mature, are quite soft. They are soft enough to be eaten whole. Life's too short to peel a shrimp.

SKATE (*see* page 25)

TURBOT
The popularity of this large flat fish has pushed its price nearly as high as that of Dover sole. In its natural state, it is not that attractive. It has a knobbly brown skin, akin to that of a frog, but it does have delicate, bright white flesh. It's also easy to handle and fillet. Overcooking kills it, so be careful. Simply poach, grill or shallow-fry it and always gently.

WINKLE
Pulling the winkle out of its shell with a long pin is great fun. The winkle is actually a sea snail. I think winkles are one of the few food items that actually benefits from plenty of vinegar.

VEGETABLES

AUBERGINE (*see* page 117)

BABY CARROT (*see* recipes, pages 96–97; *see also* Carrot, page 165, and recipes, pages 186–189)
The baby carrot usually comes to us in bunches. Some of these consist of carrots with a bit of stem, but I think they should be sold with big bunches of

fern still intact, because the fern is the best indication of freshness. These leaves will droop and rot far quicker than the root below them.

Baby carrots are expensive. Root vegetables are usually sold on weight, and a smaller carrot weighs a lot less than a great big fat one, even though the same effort has gone into growing and harvesting. However, baby carrots are usually sold prepackaged. When you grow root vegetables, you usually thin them, allowing space for each root to get bigger. If you want a baby, you don't thin, you allow them to stay all cramped up together, guaranteeing smaller and thinner carrots.

BEETROOT (see page 117 and recipes, pages 146–149)

BOK-CHOI
There is much 'choi' confusion. When is it a 'bok', and when is it a 'pak'? The simple answer is the colour. If it has white roots and green leaves it's a 'pak'. If it's green all over, it's a 'bok'. I think the green and white contrast is more attractive in 'pak', but that wouldn't stop me buying 'bok'. They both have identical crunch and juiciness.

The bok-choi is an Asian vegetable, but not all of Asia is tropical. Much of it shares the same diversity of climate as Great Britain, and because of that the bok-choi also flourishes in the UK.

Because it's Asian, most cooks will only entertain bok-choi in a stir-fry or other Eastern concoction. This is a shame. The crunch and subtle flavour of bok-choi makes it a perfect companion to virtually all meat and fish. I'm happy serving it with a Sunday roast.

BROAD BEANS (see recipes, pages 90–91)
Buying broad beans is a tricky business. The outer skin of the pod gives no indication of the quality of the bean inside. Don't worry about discolouring of the outer skin; even when it's black, it doesn't mean the bean will have been ruined. However, the size of the bumps is important. Slender bumping is what you want as this will give you a smaller and more tender bean. Big, pregnant looking pods will contain much bigger and, usually, drier beans.

There are two types of broad bean: Windsor and Longpod. The Windsor has four beans inside a short pod; the Longpod has at least double that number.

Be careful when shelling broad beans. You will note that the ends of your fingers are turning black. If you accidentally stick a blackened finger into your mouth you will know all about it; it's awful.

There are two things to remember when cooking broad beans. Firstly, don't salt the water as it will toughen the skin around the bean. Secondly, peel away the white wrinkly outer skin of the bean from the vivid green inside. It's a laborious process but worth the effort. The texture of that outer skin is not pleasant, and it is utterly tasteless.

CALABRESE (see page 117)

CANNELLINI BEAN (see page 118)

CAULIFLOWER (see page 25)

CHILLI
Chillies are capsicums, which means they are a type of pepper. There are over 150 varieties in Mexico alone, which makes classification virtually impossible. They are famed for their heat in many of the dishes of the Indian sub-continent, and also feature heavily in the foods of South-East Asia. Chillies are sometimes, but not always, sold with a heat grading. As a rule of thumb, usually the smaller they are, the hotter they are, whether green or red.

When preparing chillies, be sure to wash your hands afterwards. Touch your eye after preparing them and you will be in serious pain.

Remember to taste as you go when using chillies. They shouldn't be used just to give heat. If you use them sparingly, you will notice they have a rather fruity flavour. My advice is to prepare your chillies thus: split them and remove the seeds but don't discard them. Then remove and set aside the white pith. The flesh you're left with is milder than the pith, and the pith is milder than the seeds. So, start with the flesh: if you want more heat add the pith; if you want it hotter still, add the seeds. The chilli heat does act as a stimulant to enhance appetite, but it has also been proved to be mildly addictive, so the more you eat, the more you will crave.

If you find your chilli overbearing, water will not soothe the burning in your mouth. For help, you have to turn to a dairy product such as yoghurt, or a starchy food such as rice.

COURGETTE A courgette is a cucurbit, the same family as the marrow, cucumber, squash and melon. In fact, the courgette is a small summer squash.

This vegetable arrived quite late to our plates in the UK, and it's still not hugely popular, which I think is a shame. Most people seem to simply boil them, which isn't the best way of cooking them: the courgette, along with other cucurbits, is virtually 90 per cent water already. Much better to slice them lengthways, brush with oil and griddle them. You get more flavour this way and the slices remain firm.

COURGETTE FLOWER This is one of the true delights of a culinary summer. Many growers just lop the flowers off and throw them away. They are blind to the fact that chefs will pay a fortune for them.

I have seen many a stuffed courgette flower on a restaurant menu, but I think they are far too delicate to be stuffed. I like to dip them in a light batter and shallow-fry them. They then have a crisp outside without ruining the flavour of the whole.

We devote half a greenhouse to these beautiful things, but picking them is a nightmare. The flowers remain closed throughout the night and then open up as the sun comes over the horizon. The opening marks the beginning of the end of the flowers' very short life. If you don't pick them as they are opening they will, by early evening, have closed in on themselves and will then start to wilt.

FENNEL (*see* page 118)

FRENCH BEAN The French bean is probably the bean we recognize the most aside from tinned baked beans. It appears on at least 75 per cent of European restaurant menus. It is the very thin, long, green bean with a pointy, long, floppy nose.

They grow happily in the UK but are expensive to harvest, which is why almost all the French beans in the shops are from Kenya, where labour is cheaper.

Modern varieties are dwarf beans. They are bred to be tiny even when fully grown. Yellow ones are available, but tend to be twice the size. I prefer the round, fat variety of French bean known to me and other traders as a bobby bean. They have crunch and more juice than the anorexic French bean.

GARLIC Garlic is a member of the onion family and, like all alliums, as it ages it forms a defensive skin. There's nothing wrong with aged garlic. My only word of warning is to check for green shoots. If these shoots are protruding from your bulb then discard the whole bulb. The shoots are very bitter. Michel Roux taught me to always slice my cloves in half before cooking and to look at the shoot, or root, forming inside. If it is white and soft, leave it where it is; if it is turning green, remove it with the point of a sharp knife. I know cooks who believe they have burnt their garlic, when the bitter taste actually comes from the shoot they have failed to remove.

During the summer you should be lucky enough to get your hands on 'wet garlic'. This wetness, and it is actually wet to the touch, is simply a very new skin forming around the bulbs. This really is the only garlic that should be roasted whole.

I vigorously disapprove of garlic presses (which are really hard to clean). Everybody should learn to crush garlic. Use a lot of coarse sea salt: the abrasive flakes help break down the garlic cloves and the juice is absorbed by the salt.

Never let your garlic cook to brown. This is burnt, and the burnt flavour will infuse into everything. If you do burn garlic, throw it away, wipe your pan clean and start again. The longer you cook garlic, the milder it will get. The smaller you chop it, the stronger the flavour will be.

GLOBE ARTICHOKE (*see* page 118)

MARROW (*see* page 118)

MUSHROOMS (*see* page 26)

NEW AND SALAD POTATOES (*see* page 26 and recipes, pages 60–63; *see also* Potatoes, page 166, and recipes, pages 182–185)

ONIONS (*see* page 26)

PEAS (*see* page 26 and recipes, pages 50–53)

PEPPERS The sweet or bell pepper is thought of as a Mediterranean vegetable, but it was brought over from the Americas in the 16th century. Virtually all the peppers we get in this country are imports, but more and more are being grown in Britain, mostly under glass. I don't really like them from anywhere at all: the green are bitter, the red are sweet, and the yellow ones are a lighter tasting version of the red and green mixed together. Orange ones are just silly. Traditionally, green ones were just under-ripe red ones. Now a strain of green has been developed that will stay green even when ripe.

POTATOES (*see* page 166 and recipes, pages 182–185; *see also* New and salad potatoes, page 26 and recipes, pages 60–63)

RUNNER BEANS Originally from the New World, these beans have beautiful red flowers and grace many an allotment plot. They were originally named Scarlet Runner, 'scarlet' because of the blooms, and 'runner' from the speed with which they climb up their growing frames.

Jane Grigson confesses to not being a fan, but I like them. They can be coarse, but I enjoy that rough crispness. Buy beans as short and slender as possible and take time to run your finger over them before you buy them. The bigger they are, the rougher and tougher they get. Chop them into bite-sized chunks rather than serving them whole.

SAMPHIRE Samphire looks like a long, green, flexible root. Its texture is soft and juicy and its flavour is salty. I am unaware of any farms specializing in samphire. Mostly it's gathered as a wild plant from salty marshes near the coast. It is denser and more abundant near estuaries.

Samphire takes very little time to cook. In fact, it just needs to be thoroughly heated through. It looks beautiful with a fish balanced on top, which is why you are more likely to be able to buy it from your fishmonger than from your greengrocer.

SHALLOTS (*see* page 27)

SPINACH (*see* page 27)

SUMMER SQUASH The only difference between a winter and a summer squash is its skin. The skin forms to protect the flesh inside. In the winter the outer skin needs to be very thick indeed. Not so in the summer, when the skin is far softer and much easier to deal with. Indeed, with a summer squash there is no need to remove the skin when roasting.

The flesh inside is amazingly versatile. It will roast or mash, and squashes make superb soups.

I'm always disappointed when, in the middle of summer, I scan supermarket shelves and find nothing but butternut available as a summer squash. We had a huge influx of Australian chefs in the 1980s and I'm pretty sure it was these Aussies who popularized the butternut over here. In Australia this squash is everywhere and is as commonplace to them as a carrot is to us.

Look beyond the butternut if you can. There are lots of much better summer squashes, and three pretty ones I would urge you to try are scallop, crookneck and acorn.

SWEETCORN (*see* page 119 and recipes, pages 142–145)

SWISS CHARD (*see* recipes, pages 86–89) Swiss chard looks like rhubarb: a long thin stem with soft rounded leaves. Avoid stems wider than 7.5cm (3in). I've seen some stems over a foot wide – these are not nearly as nice as the narrower stems.

Chard is actually a type of beet, and if you look at the roots and leaves of a beetroot you will see similarities. It comes in white, green, yellow and red, and sometimes combinations of all four, known and sold as rainbow chard. Please try it. I cannot recommend this wonderful vegetable highly enough.

FRUIT

BLACKBERRY (*see* page 120 and recipes, pages 158–161)

BLUEBERRY There has never been much blueberry cultivation in the UK, but this is changing, and blueberries are becoming increasingly popular. They were always very popular in the US, but nearly died out completely at one stage. This is because there were so many growing wild that nobody saw any point in cultivating them. With huge population growth came massive picking. It wasn't until the

1920s that somebody realized that they had nearly died out, and began to grow them commercially.

Blueberries are fantastic. They are so mild, the flesh is tantalizingly soft and, unlike other berries, their juice is completely clear. The flavour intensifies when they're cooked. They are also good for you!

CHERRY (see recipes, pages 102–105) The cherry belongs to the same family as the peach, plum, almond and apricot. It can be yellow, white, pink, red or a mix of all four. Traditionally, some cherries were bred sour for cooking, some sweet. Nowadays, interbreeding has completely blurred these lines, making classification of different types difficult.

CURRANTS Currants aren't really currants. Real currants are dried fruit. The white-, red- and blackcurrants I'm discussing here are really berries.

Redcurrants have the strongest flavour, and their high pectin level is why they jam and jelly so well, although without sugar the taste can be acidic. Whitecurrants are the least acidic and usually the sweetest, but they are the hardest to cultivate. Virtually all whitecurrants grow spontaneously among redcurrants, like a kind of mad white rash!

We associate blackcurrants with juice. Funny really, because they have neither the strength nor the flavour of red, although they are very high in Vitamin C. Six little blackcurrants contain more Vitamin C than a big fat lemon.

GOOSEBERRY Gooseberries come in green, yellow or red. Some are hairy, some are smooth, but all are translucent. There is much confusion over the sourness or sweetness of a gooseberry. Indeed, at the start of the season, when I begin to sell them, a good number of the chefs will call to complain that they are too sour. There are two varieties: sour, which is for cooking, and dessert, which is sweet enough to be eaten raw. But – and this is the problem – even the dessert varieties will be sour at the start of the season. The red ones are a good dessert variety, but again these will be very sour at the start. No matter what colour they are, if they have any green on them, they will be unripe and very sour. Personally, I wouldn't take a chance and try to eat one raw; I would cook all of them.

The sharpness of a sour gooseberry sauce makes it perfect as an accompaniment for fatty game. Dessert gooseberries make great tarts or fools. I stand over the pot while they're cooking with a spoon and a sugar bowl just in case.

PLUMS (see page 120 and recipes, pages 154–157)

RASPBERRY (see recipes, pages 110–113) Look closely at a raspberry and you will notice it's covered in little white hairs. This is how it gets its name, from 'hairy' or 'raspy'. It's nothing to do with farting noises! They come in yellow, white or even black. I've never found a difference in the flavour; in fact, when I've eaten anything but red, they seem sour.

Raspberries can be frozen quite successfully. First freeze them spaced out, without touching, on a tray. Once they've frozen, mix them all together in a tub.

STRAWBERRY (see recipes, pages 106–109) The flavour of a strawberry depends on how fresh it is. A recent visit to a strawberry grower and breeder in Kent was a revelation to me. I had no idea that these fruits change flavour hourly depending on the amount of warmth or sunlight! So, please don't refrigerate them, as the cold will kill them. I don't advise washing them either, as they're very delicate. The cold water will impair their flavour and they can become waterlogged. Instead, remove the green calyx then wipe them with paper tissues.

There are hundreds of English strawberry varieties. The variety you see most is Elsanta. I don't think these strawberries are particularly bad, I just get very bored with seeing them so much. They're not grown because they're particularly tasty, but because the plant has a high fruit yield and the fruits stand up well to transit.

The three varieties I'd like you to try are Pegasus, Cambridge Favourite and Honeyeye. And if you only taste one more strawberry for the rest of your life, I beg you to get your hands on a Marie de Bois. This is the closest cultivated strawberry to the original wild *fraise de bois*, the little Alpine strawberry.

TOMATO (see recipes, pages 92–95) Please, please, don't put your tomatoes in the refrigerator.

It doesn't do the flavour or texture any good at all. Let them go a little bit soft. In fact, try leaving them out in the sunshine for a day and serve them warm. You'll get a lot more flavour.

Be careful when buying vine tomatoes; they are not necessarily better than other tomatoes. When you open a packet of tomatoes on the vine you do get a stronger tomato smell, I'll grant you that, but that smell is from the vine itself, not the fruit. Not only that; you can't get a tomato that doesn't grow on a vine. A tomato properly ripened and then picked from the vine is a lovely thing. But a bad tomato, unripe and refrigerated, is a bad tomato whether it's sold on the vine or not.

Beef tomatoes are the biggest tomatoes. They have a very thick flesh and are big enough to be stuffed, cooked, or eaten raw. Plum tomatoes are plum-shaped. They have firm flesh, fewer seeds and less liquid than other types, which makes them good for cooking, particularly in sauces. Baby plums are purely aesthetic; they have neither the strength of a plum tomato, nor the sweetness of a cherry, although they are rather pretty. There are so many types of commercially grown cherry tomatoes now that classification is almost impossible. As a rule, cherry tomatoes are usually sweeter than any other.

Of course, taste depends mostly on freshness and ripeness, but some of the most flavoursome tomatoes I've tasted have been yellow cherry. I'm in love with the 'Sun Gold' variety, a tomato I first tasted in Dorset at the home of my mate, Michael Michaux. I'm sure there are some good round or salad tomatoes, but our shops are so full of very bad ones that my advice is to avoid them all.

Through Secretts Farm I sell scores of different types of tomato, known as 'heirloom varieties', all of them virtually forgotten because their yields aren't big enough to supply national chains. They are multi-flavoured, multi-sized and multi-shaped. I won't list all the names as you are unlikely to find the exact ones I could describe anyhow, but these fruits are so popular with professional chefs in London that it can only be a matter of time before they end up in the shops. I have some that are as small as marbles and as black as coal, some that are bigger than apples and tiger-striped, and some that are small, yellow and pear-shaped.

SALADS

COS (*see* page 28)

DANDELION (*see* page 28)

FRISÉE (*see* page 28)

GEM/LITTLE GEM (*see* page 29)

ICEBERG When I was a kid, iceberg was virtually the only salad head we had. I think, mainly because of that, it's looked on as old-fashioned now and a little bit boring. That's a shame. I still love it, and see it as more retro than old-fashioned. I don't know any other salad head that is as crunchy or as juicy. I love a good prawn cocktail and I wish chefs would stick to iceberg as their salad of choice rather than opting for something more fashionable but less suited to the task.

LOLLO ROSSO Most of the lollo we see we know as 'lollo rosso'. To those of you with no linguistic capabilities, this is red lollo, although a green, or 'verde', variety is now widely available.

Lollo rosso has fallen out of favour among chefs in the know. Despite the fact that all salad creators yearn for a bit of red in their bowl (it's what my London chefs refer to as 'yer asfetix'), the lollo is virtually tasteless and slightly rubbery in texture. The green type has no more taste than the red, but has a noticeably softer leaf.

OAKLEAF This round, slightly flat, plate-shaped salad head bears a pleasing brown-green colouring. It has no discernible taste but it does bring colour to a bowl. Its leaves are soft and the neutral flavour means it will sit happily under many a dressing.

RADICCHIO (*see* page 120)

ROCKET (*see* recipes, pages 98–101) In life 'nothing is certain except death and taxes'. I'd like to amend that. Nowadays, you can be certain of death, taxes and rocket. This little green blighter is absolutely everywhere. I suspect the average person in this country eats rocket nearly as much as they do potatoes. The first time I saw rocket was as a young man in Covent Garden Market in the 1980s. In those days, it came over from Paris. I remember being amazed that such a little leaf could pack in so much heat and flavour. Back then, the only variety we had was 'broad leaf'; that is one thin stem in the middle of one rounded peppery leaf. The trendy kitchens I then supplied, always wanting to be different and one step ahead of the game, insisted on the wild variety. This type is what you nearly always get these days. Instead of a rounded leaf the wild rocket has four to five long spear-shaped leaves protruding from the stem. When I set up my own company in 1989, the wild type was impossible to get hold of. I actually had an Italian fellow growing it for me on his allotment in south-west London. By the time I moved out of Covent Garden, I was selling a minimum of 80kg (175lb) of the stuff a day! Do you know what's funny? Many of the chefs who had me track down the wild type in the first place, seeing that the rest of the world was using the wild variety, then insisted that I get them the broad-leaf variety. It's a funny thing, fashion.

Rocket is really easy to grow. In fact, it spreads like a weed. It won't handle the frost, but you can sow from early spring right through to early autumn and your rocket will be ready for picking in less than 40 days. If you cut, instead of pulling the whole thing out, it will keep growing and you can have many cuts. Experts say the second cutting is the best. Apparently, the first is too hot, and after the second it's a little too hardy. There are lots of different varieties: dark green isn't always the best, and light green doesn't mean it's weak and aged. If you let it grow really big, then you can cook it like spinach and the cooking will reduce much of the leaf's famous fieriness.

SPRING ONION (*see* page 29)

WATERCRESS (*see* page 120)

HERBS

BASIL
Many cooks advise you to rip up basil leaves with your fingers rather than cut them with a knife. Apparently the metal blade spoils the flavour.

Basil is one of the most highly scented leaves. It works well in its own right on a salad, especially if combined with the red or 'opal' basil. To me it always has a slightly metallic taste. The combination of basil and tomato was made in heaven.

Basil leaves are very soft. If you are going to use them in a cooked dish, add them at the last minute.

CHERVIL (*see* page 29)

CORIANDER (*see* page 29)

DILL (*see* page 29)

MINT (*see* page 121)

OREGANO
Oregano has a warm, heady scent. It is virtually indistinguishable from marjoram to all but the most knowledgeable cooks or herb growers. In fact, in many places it is known as wild marjoram.

I prefer dried oregano to fresh as it has far more flavour. Add it to fish dishes or chilli con carne. It is most famed as an addition to tomato sauces in Italy, and I associate it with the unmistakable aroma of pizza.

PARSLEY (*see* page 29)

ROSEMARY (*see* page 121)

SAGE (*see* page 121)

TARRAGON
I adore the aniseed taste of this herb. Tarragon is a soft-leaved but very strong herb. Be careful when you use it and remember you can always add more flavour to a dish, but you can't take it away. Get it right and the taste will make the point of your tongue tingle gently. The leaves of this herb can be ripped or cut up and tossed through salad. It is, of course, the herb used in Béarnaise sauce that matches steak so well. It is also a great accompaniment to chicken.

THYME (*see* page 121)

Sea bass

(see also page 71) Oh, what a fish! It has firm, succulent flesh and hardly any small bones; a cook's delight. It brings perfect results whether it is poached, grilled, braised or roasted. The cooked fish holds its shape well, and it's one of the best fish for serving whole. This is probably one of the main reasons why it is now so expensive.

Sea bass baked in a bag

Fish in a bag: it's so easy, it simply can't go wrong. Personally, I would take time to cut off all the fins with a pair of scissors. More than once, a sea bass has attacked me in a sort of fishy after-death experience.

125g (4½oz) butter
500g (18oz) spinach, washed and trimmed
6 tbsp finely chopped shallot
salt and pepper

4 small sea bass, gutted and scaled
4 tbsp white wine
4 bay leaves

Serves 4

Preheat the oven to 180°C/350°F/Gas 4. Melt 55g (2oz) of the butter in a large pan over a medium heat. Add the spinach and cook until it is very soft, about 4 minutes. Cool and set aside.

Melt another 55g (2oz) of the butter in a frying pan over a medium heat. Add the shallot, and sweat gently, without browning, for about 5 minutes. Stir into the spinach, season and set aside.

Wash the fish and season it inside and out. Stuff the spinach mix into the cavity.

For each fish, fold a large sheet of greaseproof paper in half and cut around the fish laid on one half to make a neat shape when opened. Make it at least 5cm (2in) larger than the fish all around. Melt the rest of the butter and brush a little on to the paper. Put a fish on one side of the paper. Pour a tablespoon of white wine over the fish and add a bay leaf. Fold over the paper to cover the fish. Make small pleats to seal the package, starting at the pointed end. Brush the outside with the rest of the butter. Place on a baking sheet.

Bake for 20–25 minutes, until the packages are brown and the fish are cooked.

Sea bass baked in salt

I've had this dish at the FishWorks restaurant and I've seen it prepared on *Masterchef*. Gently cutting through the salt crust and lifting the fish out reminds me of an archaeologist prising out a priceless artefact.

1 x 1kg (2¼ lb) sea bass, gutted and scaled
salt and pepper
1 large sprig each of tarragon, rosemary and thyme

2kg (4½ lb) coarse sea salt

Serves 2

Preheat the oven to 240°C/475°F/Gas 9. Wash the fish and dry off with kitchen paper. Lightly salt and pepper the cavity. Stuff with the herbs.

Spread half of the sea salt in a shallow, oval baking tray (just a little larger than the fish, preferably). Lay the fish in the middle of the salt. Now cover with the rest of the salt, pressing down firmly. Using a water sprayer, moisten the top lightly.

Bake the fish for about 30–40 minutes, until cooked through.

Sea bass in tomato sauce

This is truly wonderful. Make your sauce, pour it over the fish, and stick it in the oven. It just looks so good and natural when you deliver it to the middle of your dining table.

1 x 1.5kg (3lb 5oz) sea bass, gutted and scaled
juice of ½ lemon
salt and pepper
1 tbsp olive oil
1 onion, peeled and sliced
2 garlic cloves, peeled and crushed

3 tomatoes, skinned and chopped
1 tbsp chopped parsley leaves
125ml (4fl oz) dry white wine

Serves 4

Preheat the oven to 180°C/350°F/Gas 4. Wash the fish, then sprinkle inside and out with the lemon juice. Season inside and out with salt and pepper. Place in a shallow ovenproof dish big enough to hold the whole fish.

Heat the olive oil in a frying pan over a medium heat and fry the onion and garlic until softened but not brown, about 6–8 minutes. Add the chopped tomato with the parsley, and simmer gently for 4–5 minutes. Stir in the wine and pour this mixture over the fish in the ovenproof dish.

Bake for about 40 minutes, until the fish is cooked. The flesh will flake easily, if ready, when tested with a knife.

Crab

(see also page 70) I have very early and delightful memories of this succulent crustacean. When I was a wee lad, we would regularly catch the train to visit my grandmother. Outside the station was a seafood stall and every now and then my mother would buy a dressed crab from this stall to take to Nanny's house. Writing this has brought the smell right back.

Crab tart

This tart is simply delicious. It looks great and it is bursting with crab. I could eat lots and lots.

PASTRY
250g (9oz) plain flour
a pinch of salt
½ tsp cayenne pepper
125g (4½oz) butter, cold and cubed
30g (1¼oz) Cheddar, finely grated
1 medium egg yolk

FILLING
3 medium eggs

2 tsp lemon juice
1 tbsp Worcestershire sauce
250g (9oz) crab meat
125ml (4fl oz) double cream
2 tbsp chopped chives
salt and pepper

Serves 4–6

For the pastry, put the flour, salt, cayenne pepper, butter and cheese in a food processor. Whizz until the mixture is like breadcrumbs. Add the egg yolk and whizz briefly until a dough forms. If it is too dry, add a tablespoon of water. Knead on a floured surface quickly. Cover with clingfilm and chill in the refrigerator for 30 minutes.

Preheat the oven to 200°C/400°F/Gas 6.

Roll out the pastry on a floured work surface and use to line a 23cm (9in) flan tin. Prick the base with a fork. Use scrunched-up foil to line the sides of the pastry and bake blind for 15 minutes. Remove from the oven, discard the foil, and reduce the oven heat to 190°C/375°F/Gas 5.

Beat the eggs with the lemon juice and Worcestershire sauce, then stir in the crab meat, cream and chives. Check the seasoning. Spoon the mixture into the pastry case and bake for 25–30 minutes.

This tart can be served hot or cold.

Crab cakes

Who can resist crab cakes? My only word of warning is to make sure you go through your crabmeat very carefully. Nobody wants to break their teeth on the old house of a dead crustacean.

350g (12oz) white crab meat
55g (2oz) soft white breadcrumbs
1 tbsp finely chopped spring onion
2 tbsp finely chopped chives
2 tbsp chopped parsley leaves
1 tsp mustard powder
1 medium egg, beaten
3 tbsp mayonnaise

1 tbsp Worcestershire sauce
a pinch of cayenne pepper
salt and pepper
a little plain flour
30g (1¼ oz) butter
1 tbsp vegetable oil

Serves 4

In a large bowl mix together the crab, breadcrumbs, onions, chives, parsley and mustard powder. In a separate bowl, mix the egg with the mayonnaise and Worcestershire sauce. Mix this into the dry ingredients. Season with cayenne, salt and pepper. Chill for about an hour.

Shape the crab mixture into four cakes and flour them lightly. Heat the butter and oil in a large frying pan over a medium heat. Fry the cakes on both sides until brown, about 2½ minutes on each side. Drain on kitchen paper and serve hot.

Devilled crab

These are little pots of fiery crab. Prepare them in advance and stick them in the oven when needed for a perfect dinner-party starter.

40g (1½oz) butter
1 tbsp plain flour
175ml (6fl oz) single cream
1 tbsp mild mustard
4 pinches cayenne pepper
1 tbsp Worcestershire sauce

salt and pepper
350g (12oz) white crab meat
2 medium hard-boiled eggs, shelled and chopped
55g (2oz) fresh white breadcrumbs

Serves 4

Preheat the oven to 200°C/400°F/Gas 6. Melt 30g (1¼oz) of the butter in a small pan. Blend in the flour and cook for 2 minutes. Gradually add the single cream, stirring all the time, and simmer gently for 5 minutes. Whisk in the mustard, 1 pinch of the cayenne pepper, the Worcestershire sauce, and some salt and pepper

Fold in the crab meat and chopped egg, then share this mixture out between four ramekins on a baking sheet. Top with the breadcrumbs and the remaining cayenne pepper. Add the remaining butter in small cubes.

Bake for about 20 minutes, until golden brown.

Swiss chard

(*see also* page 74) Sometimes known just as chard, this definitely makes it into my top ten most-loved vegetables. Both leaves and stem are very tender. The stem delivers a beautiful crunch and flavoursome juice, and both take hardly any cooking at all. The leaves will cook quicker than the stem and you may want to separate them before cooking. I don't bother.

Chard and sausage pie

A steaming pie brought to a table smacks of farmhouse kitchens. If you've never made a pie, this is a good one to start with. It has few ingredients, so it's easy to achieve the prized pie result with minimum effort.

PASTRY
300g (10½oz) plain flour
a pinch of salt
150g (5½oz) butter, cold and cubed
1 medium egg, beaten with 1 tbsp cold water

FILLING
1kg (2¼ lb) Swiss chard, washed and trimmed
salt and pepper

55g (2oz) butter
freshly grated nutmeg
3 garlic cloves, peeled and crushed
300g (10½oz) good-quality sausages, skinned
  and chopped
4 tbsp chopped parsley leaves
2 tbsp crème fraîche

Serves 6

To make the pastry, put the flour, salt and cubed butter in a food processor. Whizz until the mixture looks like breadcrumbs. Set aside 1 tbsp of the egg and water mixture. With the processor on, pour the rest of the liquid in slowly to make a dough. Use a little more water if you need to. Knead gently on a floured surface to make a smooth dough. Wrap in clingfilm and chill in the refrigerator for 30 minutes.

Preheat the oven to 190°C/375°F/Gas 5.

For the filling, separate the leaves from the stems of the chard. Shred the leaves and set aside. Chop the stems into quite small bits. Put a little salted water in a large saucepan and bring to the boil. Tip in the chard stems and blanch for 5 minutes, then drain well. Put half the butter in the empty saucepan. Melt and add the blanched stems and the shredded leaves. Cover and cook over a high heat for about another 5 minutes, until the leaves have wilted right down. Season with salt, pepper and nutmeg. Drain well.

In a frying pan over a medium heat, melt the remaining butter. When it stops sizzling, add the garlic and sausage, and cook until well browned. Add the parsley and take off the heat. Mix well with the cooked chard, along with the crème fraîche.

Roll out the pastry on a floured surface and use just over half to line a tart tin 20–23cm (8–9in) across. Wet the edges with water. Fill the pastry with the chard mixture and make it level. Use the rest of the pastry to cover the pie. Press down the edges to seal and make a hole in the middle of the pie. Brush all over with the reserved egg.

Bake for about 30 minutes, until brown and golden.

Swiss chard bake

When cooked like this, Swiss chard is right up there with my favourite vegetables of the world.

1kg (2¼ lb) Swiss chard, washed and trimmed
salt and pepper
butter
150ml (5fl oz) vegetable or chicken stock

300ml (10fl oz) double cream
freshly grated nutmeg

Serves 6

Preheat the oven to 170°C/325°F/Gas 3.

Cut the leaves of the chard away from the stalks. Shred the leaves and cut the stalks into 3cm (1¼in) lengths, keeping them separate.

Bring a large pan of salted water to the boil. When boiling, add the stalks and cook for about 4 minutes. Then add the leaves and cook for a further 2 minutes. Drain well.

Put the chard into a large, ovenproof buttered gratin dish and season.

In a small pan, heat the stock and cream together until simmering. Season with a few gratings of nutmeg, and some salt and pepper. Pour over the prepared chard and bake for about an hour, until brown and bubbling.

Chard-stuffed pancakes

There's something about making pancakes that really reminds me of my childhood. These ones are absolutely packed with flavour.

PANCAKES
125g (4½oz) plain flour
a pinch of salt
2 medium eggs, beaten
2 tbsp melted butter, plus extra for frying
2 tbsp whisky
150ml (5fl oz) milk
150ml (5fl oz) water

FILLING
750g (1lb 10oz) Swiss chard, washed and trimmed
175ml (6fl oz) crème fraiche

salt and pepper
60g (2¼ oz) butter
1 small onion, chopped
2 cloves garlic, chopped
100g (3½oz) chestnut mushrooms, chopped
1 tbsp plain flour
250ml (9fl oz) milk
35g (1¼ oz) anchovy fillets, chopped
grated nutmeg
cayenne pepper

Serves 6

In a large bowl, mix the pancake ingredients together in the order given, adding the liquid slowly until you have a smooth batter. Brush a medium frying pan with a little extra butter, heat over a medium heat and pour in enough mixture to just cover the base of the pan. When large bubbles start showing, turn the pancakes over to cook through. Put the cooked pancake on a plate, and keep making pancakes until the batter is used up. This should make about 12 pancakes. Set aside.

Preheat the oven to 190°C/375°F/Gas 5.

Cut the leaves of the chard from the stalks. Shred the leaves; chop the stalks quite small and keep them separate. Bring a large pan of salted water to the boil. When boiling add the chopped stalks and cook for about 4 minutes, then add the leaves and cook for a further 2 minutes. Drain well. Return to the pan and add 50ml (2fl oz) of the crème fraîche with some salt and pepper.

Over the medium heat, in a medium pan, melt the butter then add the onion and garlic and sweat gently for about 5 minutes. Add the mushrooms, cook for 2 minutes, then add the flour. Stir in and cook for another 2 minutes. Add the milk and remaining cream and simmer gently for 10 minutes. Now add the anchovies, using as many as suits your taste. Season with a few gratings of nutmeg, some cayenne, salt and pepper.

Stuff the pancakes with the creamed chard. Roll up and place in a large ovenproof buttered gratin dish. Pour the sauce over the pancakes, and bake in the preheated oven for about 30 minutes.

Broad beans

(see also page 72) Amazingly, the broad bean is the only bean native to Europe. Every other bean was brought to us from the New World. I think the broad is my favourite bean, as I love that mealy texture.

When cooking, don't ever salt the water, as this will toughen the skin around the bean. And do make the effort to peel away the white, wrinkly outer skin of the bean from the vivid green inside. I know it's a laborious process, but it's well worth the effort. The texture of the outer skin is not pleasant, and utterly tasteless.

Broad beans with ham

This is a clever adaptation of 'French peas'. It tastes just as good cold the next day.

1 tbsp vegetable oil
1 onion, peeled and finely chopped
75g (2¾ oz) cooked ham, finely diced
350g (12oz) podded broad beans
2 little gem lettuces, sliced
100ml (3½ fl oz) vegetable or chicken stock

3 tbsp crème fraîche
salt and pepper
2 tbsp chopped chervil

Serves 4

Heat the oil in a large saucepan over a medium heat. Fry the onion and ham until soft but not browned, about 5 minutes. Add the beans and lettuce, cover the pan and cook for about 6 minutes, giving it the odd stir.

Now add the stock to the pan with the crème fraîche. Season and cook over a very low heat for 20 minutes, stirring occasionally. At the end of the cooking time, gently stir in the chervil.

Broad bean and chervil pâté

This is simple and truly fantastic. Serve spread on crostini.

400g (14oz) podded broad beans
250g (9oz) cream cheese
15g (½ oz) chervil
1 tbsp olive oil

finely grated zest and juice of 1 lemon
salt and pepper

Serves 4

Cook the broad beans in boiling water (no salt!) for 3 minutes. Drain in a colander, running cold water over the hot beans. When cool, slip off and discard the skins.

Place the beans, cheese, chervil, oil, zest and only half the lemon juice, in a food processor. Season, then whizz to quite a rough paste. Taste to check the seasoning, adding more lemon juice if needed.

Tomatoes

Tomatoes (*see also* page 75) Many people tell me that tomatoes abroad taste so much better than the ones we get here, implying that you can't get a decent tomato in the UK. That's just not true. We have many superb tomatoes in the UK. The reason that people think tomatoes abroad are better is because they probably eat them in the middle of summer, just picked, and most certainly not refrigerated. Yet, curiously, people in the UK buy an imported tomato, picked unripe, refrigerated, and flown halfway around the world to reach us, and somehow think that these tomatoes must be home grown and bear no comparison to the lovely ones they ate on holiday. Get real! A decent tomato allowed to ripen on the vine is as good in Britain as it is in Spain or Italy.

Green tomato chutney

Do you like cheese? This is the perfect accompaniment. Many people make chutneys and give them to friends as presents. I have never, ever, given any of this away.

500g (18oz) cooking apples, peeled, cored
   and chopped
2kg (4½lb) green tomatoes, washed and
   thoroughly chopped
500g (18oz) onions, peeled and chopped
4 garlic cloves, peeled and crushed

2 green chillies, seeds in, chopped
1 tsp salt
3 tbsp pickling spice
600ml (1 pint) cider vinegar
500g (18oz) granulated or pickling sugar

Makes about 1.5kg (3lb 5oz)

Put the apples, tomatoes, onions, garlic, chillies and salt in a preserving pan. Tie the pickling spice in a piece of muslin and add to the pan. Pour in half of the vinegar and simmer for an hour without a lid, until the chutney is very thick. Be sure to stir often.

Preheat the oven to its lowest setting, and sterilize the jars (*see* page 65).

In a microwave, dissolve the sugar in the remaining vinegar and add to the chutney. Simmer for another 1½ hours until the chutney is really thick, stirring every now and then. Remove the bag of spices and bottle the chutney into the warm sterilized jars. Seal each jar with a wax disc and, when cold, cover with a cellophane cover and a lid. Store in a dark place for at least a month before using.

Stuffed beef tomatoes

That lovely tomato pulp oozing through the stuffing is amazingly refreshing. I'm a big anchovy fan; use more of them if you like them too.

6 large ripe beef tomatoes
2 onions, peeled and chopped
4 tbsp olive oil, plus extra for drizzling
3 garlic cloves, peeled and crushed
100g (3½oz) flaked almonds
6 anchovy fillets, finely chopped
75g (2¾oz) long-grain rice, boiled and drained

15g (½oz) mint leaves, chopped
15g (½oz) parsley leaves, chopped
3 tbsp sultanas
salt and pepper
3 tbsp fresh white breadcrumbs

Serves 4

Preheat the oven to 190°C/375°F/Gas 5. Cut the tomatoes in half, remove the seeds and pulp with a spoon. Leave the tomato shells to drain, upside-down, on kitchen paper. Chop the tomato pulp, and set aside.

In a large frying pan, fry the onion in the oil over a medium heat for about 5 minutes, until soft and lightly browned. Add the garlic, flaked almonds and anchovies and fry for another minute.

Remove from the heat and stir in the just-cooked rice, half the tomato pulp, the herbs and sultanas. Season well.

Place the tomato shells in an ovenproof dish, just large enough to hold them. Fill with the stuffing. Pour 150ml (5fl oz) boiling water around them and bake for about 20 minutes.

Remove from the oven, sprinkle over the breadcrumbs and drizzle over a little extra olive oil. Put back into the oven for another 20 minutes. Serve just warm or at room temperature.

Three tomato and onion salad

There are now more tomatoes on the market than ever before, and the trend looks set to continue. I have more than 15 varieties at my farm, and the London chefs can't seem to get enough of them.

200g (7oz) red cherry tomatoes, halved
200g (7oz) yellow cherry tomatoes, halved
200g (7oz) beef tomatoes, chopped
1 bunch spring onions, finely sliced
1 red onion, peeled and finely sliced

DRESSING
1 tbsp red wine vinegar
6 tbsp chopped parsley
a pinch of caster sugar
salt and pepper

Serves 4

Whisk the dressing ingredients together in a bowl.

Mix the tomatoes and onion together in a large bowl. Pour over the dressing, and leave to sit for half an hour before serving.

Baby carrots (*see also* page 71) Baby carrots are lighter than winter carrots, with less crunch under the tooth. However, they are delightfully sweet and tender, and much more attractive on a plate when used whole than a chopped big carrot.

Glazed baby carrots

This is so easy. The honey brings out the natural sweetness in the carrots, raising them to another level.

500g (18oz) baby carrots, scrubbed
55g (2oz) butter
1 tbsp honey

salt and pepper

Serves 4

Leave about 3cm (1¼in) stalk on the carrots. If small, leave whole. If larger, cut into two or three pieces.

Place the carrots in a pan wide enough to take them in a single layer. Almost cover them with water, adding the butter, honey and seasoning. Bring to the boil, and cook for about 10–13 minutes, until the carrots are tender and the liquid has reduced to a thick glaze.

Carrot and apple coleslaw

The tangy bite of apple is beautifully refreshing. This is so easy to make and the longer you leave it in the refrigerator, the more the flavours blend together.

400g (14oz) baby carrots, scrubbed and finely grated
2 Cox's apples, cored and thinly sliced
1 tbsp lemon juice
1 large orange

DRESSING
6 tbsp vegetable oil
1 tbsp lemon juice

1 garlic clove, peeled and crushed
4 tbsp natural yoghurt
1 tbsp chopped tarragon leaves
1 tbsp chopped chives
salt and pepper

Serves 4

Put the carrots in a large bowl, and add the apples. Sprinkle with lemon juice, and mix well. With a sharp knife, remove the skin and pith from the orange. Over the bowl, to catch the juice, carefully separate the segments and drop them into the bowl.

Put the dressing ingredients in a bowl and whisk together. Pour over the vegetables and fruit, and mix carefully. Check the seasoning before serving.

Rocket

(see also page 76) Rarely will you find a salad leaf with so many names: *roquet*, *roquette*, *arugula*, *rucola* or rocket! I suppose it became so popular because it has so much flavour. It's also very hardy and will stand up to the most aggressive of dressings. I think my favourite way of serving it is simple: Parmesan, olive oil and a bit of lemon.

Although it's native to the Mediterranean, I'm willing to bet a tenner that most of the stuff you're sampling comes from Israel.

Rocket, fennel and orange salad

This is a nice combination on a summer's day. Hot rocket, aniseedy fennel and the sweet citrus juice of orange together cleanse the palate beautifully.

2 large oranges
1 medium head fennel, trimmed
1 small red onion, peeled and finely sliced
55g (2oz) rocket leaves, washed

DRESSING
15g (½oz) black olives, stoned
2 sun-dried tomatoes in oil

1 garlic clove, peeled and crushed
1 tbsp chopped parsley
6 tbsp extra virgin olive oil
2 tbsp balsamic vinegar
salt and pepper

Serves 4

For the dressing, place the olives and sun-dried tomatoes in a food processor with the garlic, parsley and 1 tbsp oil. Whizz to make a smooth paste. Transfer to a small bowl and whisk in the remaining oil, the vinegar and some seasoning.

With a sharp knife, remove the skin and all the pith from the oranges. Then carefully, over a large bowl to catch the juice, remove segments of orange from the fruit. Drop the segments into the bowl.

Discard the outer layer from the fennel, and slice the rest very thinly. Add to the oranges with the onion and rocket. Pour the dressing over and mix well.

Rocket and parsley salad

Your tastebuds will dance like crazy with the tastes in this salad: garlicky, peppery, sweet, and tangy.

2 garlic cloves, peeled and halved
4 slices good bread, crusts removed
3 tbsp olive oil
100g (3½oz) rocket leaves, washed
55g (2oz) baby spinach leaves
25g (1oz) flat-leaf parsley leaves
55g (2oz) Parmesan, shaved

DRESSING
1 tbsp pesto

2 garlic cloves, peeled and crushed
1 tsp mild mustard
5 tbsp olive oil
2 tsp balsamic vinegar
salt and pepper
a squeeze of lemon juice

Serves 6

Preheat the oven to 190°C/375°F/Gas 5. For the dressing, whisk all the ingredients together. Taste and adjust the seasoning.

Rub the garlic cloves over the bread and cut the bread into small cubes. Put on a baking tray, pour over the olive oil, and stir. Bake for about 10 minutes, until golden brown. Cool and set aside.

To serve, mix the rocket, spinach and parsley in a salad bowl. Mix the cooled bread cubes with the salad and add the dressing. Top with the shavings of Parmesan.

Cherries

(*see also* page 75) When I was a kid my grandparents lived upstairs. My finest memories are of weekend shopping with them for the first cherries and strawberries of the season. Afterwards, I would sit at the kitchen table with Granddad picking the stalks from the cherries, supposedly stoning them for my Nan's tart, but eating most of them instead. Many of the cherries hung from stalks in pairs and whenever we heard anybody coming, we would hang these pairs over our ears like big earrings and try to carry on stoning as if it were a perfectly reasonable thing to do.

I still enjoy cherry stoning, but I think it's worth getting yourself a little machine. You know what I mean, they are like a stapler. You press down on the top and a blunt point comes up through the cherry, hopefully with the stone on the end of it. It's a seriously messy job – the juice goes everywhere and it does stain. I suggest you use rubber gloves. I don't, I sport my stained hands like culinary war wounds.

I love that soft flesh with the crisp outside and that unique flavour of sweet and sharp acidity.

Hot cherries with fried custard bread

This is a favourite of the kids. Stoning the cherries is the most laborious bit: if you don't do this properly, you will end up with a huge dental bill.

2 medium eggs
250ml (9fl oz) single cream
55g (2oz) caster sugar
4 slices good white bread, about 1cm (½in) thick

400g (14oz) cherries, stoned
40g (1½oz) butter

Serves 4

Beat the eggs with the cream and 1 tbsp of the sugar.

Put the slices of bread (crusts on or off, you choose) in a large flat container. Pour the cream mixture over the bread. The slices should all be evenly soaked. Turn the slices over a couple of times to make sure they soak up all the liquid.

Put the cherries in a pan with the rest of the sugar. Slowly bring up to simmering point. Leave over a very low heat while you fry the bread.

In a large frying pan, melt the butter over a medium heat. Add the slices of bread and fry on both sides until crisp and golden.

Put each slice of bread on a plate and pour the cherries and their juice evenly over. Serve very hot. (A scoop of vanilla ice-cream on top works very well.)

Cherry flan

Oh yes! This looks very pretty on the Sunday tea table. If you make a very shallow flan, you may have some mixture left over. Don't worry about it, use it to make yourself some little individual ones.

PASTRY
175g (6oz) plain flour
1 tbsp caster sugar
a pinch of salt
125g (4½oz) butter, cold and cubed
2–3 tbsp cold water

FILLING
3 medium eggs

300ml (10fl oz) double cream
55g (2oz) caster sugar
1 tsp vanilla essence
500g (18oz) cherries, stoned

Serves 6–8

To make the pastry, in a food processor, whizz the flour, sugar, salt and butter until the mixture looks like breadcrumbs. Slowly add the cold water until the mixture forms a dough. Remove the dough from the machine and knead lightly until smooth. Cover with clingfilm and chill in the refrigerator for an hour.

Preheat the oven to 220°C/425°F/Gas 7. Roll out the dough on a floured surface and use to line a 25cm (10in) loose-bottomed flan tin. Prick the base all over with a fork. Line the edges with scrunched-up foil, and blind-bake for 10 minutes. Remove the foil and bake for another 15 minutes. Remove the pastry case from the oven and turn the oven temperature down to 180°C/350°F/Gas 4.

For the filling, beat the eggs in a large bowl with the cream, sugar and vanilla essence, until blended.

Place the stoned cherries in the cooked pastry shell. Gently pour over the filling mixture and bake for about 30 minutes, until the custard is set.

This can be served warm or cold.

Cherry and chocolate cake

Do you make cakes? Are you scared of them? You shouldn't be. Follow these instructions and, I promise you, you will become a top cook overnight.

55g (2oz) blanched almonds, toasted
55g (2oz) plain flour
125g (4½oz) good-quality plain dark chocolate
3 tbsp water
3 medium eggs, separated
125g (4½oz) butter, softened
125g (4½oz) caster sugar

TOPPING
400g (14oz) cherries, stoned

4 tbsp rum or brandy
chocolate shavings

GANACHE
225g (8oz) good-quality plain dark chocolate, broken
    into pieces
450ml (16fl oz) double cream

Serves 8

For the topping, place the stoned cherries in a small bowl with 3 tbsp of the rum or brandy. Leave to soak overnight.

Preheat the oven to 180°C/350°F/Gas 4. Grease a 23cm (9in) springform tin and line with baking parchment. Whizz the almonds and flour together in a food processor until the nuts are finely ground.

Melt the 125g (4½oz) chocolate with the water in a bowl over simmering water. Take off the heat and beat in the egg yolks with the remaining tablespoon of rum or brandy. Set aside.

Beat the butter and sugar together until light and fluffy. Stir in the chocolate mix, then gently fold in the flour/almond mix. Whisk the egg whites until soft peaks form. Gently fold this into the cake mix.

Pour into the prepared tin and bake for 30–35 minutes, until cooked through. Remove from the oven and leave in the tin for 10 minutes. Turn out of the tin on to a wire rack and leave to cool completely.

For the ganache, put the chocolate pieces in a large bowl. Bring the cream to the boil and pour over the chocolate. Leave for about 5 minutes, by which time the chocolate should have melted. Mix together well and leave to cool.

With an electric mixer, beat the ganache until lighter in colour and very thick. Put the cold cake back in the clean springform tin. Pour over the cherries and alcohol. Spoon over the ganache, and smooth the surface. Cover with clingfilm and chill for at least 2 hours before serving. Remove the outside of the tin before doing so.

Decorate with chocolate shavings. Simply use a potato peeler along the side of a bar of chocolate to make these.

Strawberries

(*see also* page 75) This is my favourite fruit – plump, soft flesh awash with juice and a floral-honey flavour. I have fond memories of hunting for the first summer strawberries with my grandparents on Rye Lane, Peckham. We would have a special strawberry tea that day and Granddad and I would secretly steal as many as we could without my grandmother noticing. It terrifies me to think that children nowadays grow up thinking that strawberries taste of the flavourless imported varieties that stock our shelves 12 months of the year.

Strawberry tartlets

The jelly glaze on top of these tartlets does the trick. It makes the top shiny and heightens the strawberry flavour.

PASTRY
200g (7oz) plain flour
a pinch of salt
100g (3½oz) butter, cold and cubed
2 tbsp caster sugar
1 medium egg yolk, beaten with 1 tbsp cold water

CUSTARD CREAM
1 medium egg yolk
25g (1oz) caster sugar

1½ tbsp plain flour
125ml (4fl oz) milk
15g (½oz) butter
1 tsp vanilla essence

TOPPING
500g (18oz) strawberries, hulled
150g (5½oz) redcurrant jelly

Makes 20

To make the pastry, whizz the flour, salt, butter and sugar together in a food processor until it looks like breadcrumbs. Gradually add enough of the egg mixture to form a dough. Remove the dough from the processor, and knead lightly until smooth. Cover with clingfilm and chill in the refrigerator for an hour.

Preheat the oven to 190°C/375°F/Gas 5. To make the custard cream, put the egg yolk and sugar in a bowl and beat well until smooth and creamy. Mix in the flour. Heat the milk to just under boiling point. Add the milk to the egg mix, whisking well all the time. Return the mix to the milk pan and, over a gentle heat, bring to the boil, stirring all the time. Cook very gently for 2 minutes. Remove from the heat and stir in the butter and vanilla essence. Pour into a small bowl, cover the surface with clingfilm, and leave to chill.

Roll out half the pastry on a floured surface. Cut out 10 x 7.5cm (3in) rounds. Put each into an ungreased dip in a fairy cake tray and press in. Prick the bases with a fork. Chill for 30 minutes. Repeat with the rest of the pastry.

Bake the chilled tartlet cases for about 10 minutes. Remove from the oven and leave to sit for 2 minutes before removing them carefully from the tin and setting on a wire cooling tray.

When the pastries are cold, spoon about 2 tsp of custard mixture into each. Top with a few strawberries (whole or sliced – you decide – they're your tarts). Melt the redcurrant jelly in a small pan for a couple of minutes. Leave to cool slightly, then brush the jelly over the strawberries to finish. Leave to set for at least 10 minutes before serving.

Strawberry pavlova

One mouthful of this reassures me that there is a God looking after our wellbeing. The light meringue and concentrated fruit flavour taste fantastic.

4 medium egg whites
250g (9oz) caster sugar
1 tsp white wine vinegar
1 tsp cornflour
1 tsp vanilla essence

200g (7oz) redcurrants, stalks removed
3 tbsp icing sugar
350ml (12fl oz) double cream

Serves 8

TOPPING
500g (18oz) strawberries, hulled and halved

Preheat the oven to 150°C/300°F/Gas 2. On a sheet of baking parchment, mark a 23cm (9in) circle with a pencil. Whisk the egg whites to stiff peaks with a hand mixer. Whisk in the sugar, a tablespoon at a time, until a stiff, glossy meringue is formed. Whisk in the vinegar, cornflour and vanilla essence.

Place the marked paper on a baking sheet, pencilled-side down. Spoon the meringue into the marked circle and spread to the edges, making a dip in the middle of the meringue so the outside edge is higher.

Bake for 1 hour, or until the meringue is pale and hard to the touch. Turn off the oven and leave the pavlova inside until cold.

Chop up 100g (3½oz) of the strawberries, and mix with half the redcurrants and 2 tbsp of the icing sugar. Put in a small pan and gently heat up. Don't cook the berries; just warm them up so the sugar melts, the juices come out and the redcurrants burst. Push through a sieve and leave to cool.

When ready to serve, whip the cream with the remaining icing sugar. Pile the whipped cream into the cold meringue shell. Mix the remaining fruit together and pile on top of the cream. Pour the sweet sauce evenly over the fruit.

Raspberries

(see also page 75) As a passionate Englishman, it hurts me to say that the best raspberries can be found in Scotland. Contrary to popular belief, most soft fruit does not enjoy a scorchingly hot summer.

Raspberry brûlée

The first thing is, everybody loves to play with the little blow-torches. I wouldn't tell anybody their brûlée's got raspberries in it. Don't spoil the surprise.

600ml (1 pint) double cream
1 vanilla pod, split lengthways
4 medium egg yolks
100g (3½oz) caster sugar
about 36 raspberries

Serves 6

Preheat the oven to 150°C/300°F/Gas 2. Place the cream and vanilla pod in a small saucepan over a low heat and very, very gently heat to almost boiling point. Remove from the heat and remove the pod.

Beat the egg yolks with half the sugar in a bowl, then slowly pour the hot cream over the eggs, whisking all the time.

Divide the raspberries between six ramekins. Pour the custard over the fruit, carefully and equally.

Put the filled ramekins in a roasting tin. Pour enough boiling water into the tin to come halfway up the sides of the ramekins. Place the tin in the oven for an hour, or until the custard is just set. Remove the ramekins from the tin and leave to cool. Refrigerate overnight.

A couple of hours before serving, sprinkle the remaining sugar evenly over the custards. Using a gas gun, very carefully grill the sugar to form a caramel. Keep the flame moving so as not to burn the sugar. Alternatively, heat under a medium grill. Allow to cool and chill before serving.

Berries with warm sabayon glaze

You can serve your berries *au naturel* if you like, I won't complain; but for a dinner party this glaze just makes them a little more special.

250g (9oz) raspberries
300g (10½oz) mixed summer berries
4 medium egg yolks
125ml (4fl oz) sweet dessert wine

55g (2oz) caster sugar
icing sugar, to decorate

Serves 4

Arrange the washed berries in four medium ramekins or on four small dessert plates.

Place a large bowl over a pan of simmering water (the bowl should not touch the water). Put the egg yolks, wine and sugar into the bowl. Now whisk like mad manually until thick and fluffy, or be clever and use an electric hand-mixer (this takes almost as long but hurts less). About 4–5 minutes should do it.

Spoon the sabayon evenly over the fruit. Sift over a little icing sugar. Now light a gas gun and lightly colour the glaze. Alternatively, heat under a medium grill. Serve immediately.

Raspberry mousse

This is the proper way of making a fruit mousse. Master the technique and you will be moussing for the rest of your life. You'll have more mousses than a Canadian pine forest!

450g (1lb) raspberries, plus extra to decorate
1 x 11g sachet powdered gelatine
4 tbsp cold water
125g (4½oz) cream cheese

55g (2oz) caster sugar
2 medium egg whites
150ml (5fl oz) whipping cream, plus extra to decorate

Serves 6

Force the raspberries through a sieve to make a purée. Set aside.

Sprinkle the gelatine over the water in a small bowl, and leave to soak for a couple of minutes. Place the bowl over a pan of simmering water to heat up gently, stirring until the gelatine has dissolved. Take off the heat.

Beat the cream cheese and sugar together until smooth, then stir in the raspberry purée. Pour the dissolved gelatine into the cream cheese mix, whisking all the time. Leave to stand until the mixture shows signs of setting.

Whisk the egg whites to stiff peaks, then, in a separate bowl, whip the cream to soft peaks. Fold the whipped cream into the fruit mix, then fold in the beaten egg whites.

Divide the mixture between six glass dishes, and chill until set. Decorate with extra cream and fruit.

Autumn

Autumn ingredients

FISH

BRILL Brill is a very decent fish, although for some reason it's not one of the trendies. It's actually a lot cheaper than, and not a bad substitute for, turbot. It's as easy to fillet as a turbot, its flesh is a little softer, and it stands up to cooking for a little longer.

COD (*see* recipes, pages 134–137) Cod may traditionally be our favourite fish, but there is now much controversy surrounding its catching and eating. New fishing techniques and the use of trawlers bring in bigger and bigger catches, severely depleting stocks, and cod are now widely acknowledged to be a threatened species in the North Sea, the Baltic and the North Atlantic. Once fishermen landed cod as heavy as 50kg (110lb); now the norm is only 5kg (11lb) as the fish have little opportunity to grow and mature.

I'm quite optimistic, though, as cod are efficient and prolific breeders and reach maturity quite quickly. If left alone for a while, as recommended by certain advisory bodies, stocks should increase to healthy levels. If you'd like to continue eating cod but want to maintain a clear conscience, consider buying only line-caught cod from sustainable waters or organically farmed cod, which is now available from the Shetland Isles. This is more expensive, but the fish is finer, as the cod don't suffer the bruising that those caught in trawler nets suffer.

COLEY (*see* page 24)

CRAB (*see* page 70 and recipes, pages 82–85)

EEL Eels used to be a particular favourite in working-class London, at least in my grandparents' generation. Pots of jellied eels were never a favourite of mine, but, served stewed and piping hot with parsley sauce, eels can be a delight. The flesh of the eel is firm and very rich, and it is very good cold, served with a mixture of horseradish and beetroot.

Get your fishmonger to prepare your eel for you. They can grow up to 90cm (3ft) long, and although the skin, black on top and silver underneath, is attractive, it is difficult to remove – and very messy.

GREY MULLET The only mullet native to Britain is the grey mullet. It is a particularly hardy fish and can survive in some very polluted water. This is its downfall (well, as a food anyway), as the taste very much depends on where it was caught. If it was caught in a harbour mouth, it can taste a bit muddy.

HALIBUT You hardly ever see these huge, deep-sea fish whole. They can grow up to 1.8m (6ft) in length and weigh well over 100kg (220lb). They are very meaty indeed, with dense, firm white flesh. In the shops, you nearly always see them sold as steaks. At the fat end of the tail these steaks can be enormous, and at the thin end you get too much bone, so aim for the middle. The only issue I have with halibut steaks is that they can be a bit dry, so I think it's best to poach or braise them in liquid.

JOHN DORY (*see* page 24)

LANGOUSTINE (*see* page 24)

OYSTER I live in Whitstable, on the Kent coast, which is famed for its oysters. At the right time of year a trip to the oyster sheds is a real treat for me.

That old saying regarding only eating oysters when there is an 'R' in the month is a good rule to follow. In other months, the oyster tends to be a bit milky. Oysters must be bought alive: a dead or old one eaten raw can make you very sick indeed. Hold your oyster in the palm of your hand; it should feel heavy. Tap it; it should sound full, with no hollowness. Most oysters are shut tight; if they are open they should close when you touch them.

Oysters come in two types: 'natives' and 'rocks'. Most connoisseurs agree that natives have a finer flavour. Oyster shell shapes will adapt to their surroundings, but generally a native is round and a rock oblong.

PLAICE (*see* page 25)

PRAWNS (*see* recipes, pages 138–141) Don't bother buying prawns out of their shells; there is no comparison in the flavour. Even in their shells, too many of the prawns we buy have been frozen. Look at their eyes; those little black things which, if they've been frozen, look shrivelled rather than rounded – as I suspect my eyes would look if you stuck me in the freezer.

SPRAT This little fish is very oily, but reasonably priced. It is related to the herring, but is only about 15cm (6in) long. The sprat can be cooked whole – just remove the scales first. Don't worry, they come off easily and can be removed with the blunt end of a knife. If you really must fillet them, you can manage this with your fingers. Fry or grill them whole.

GAME

DUCK (*see* recipes, pages 122–125) The amount of fat on a duck means that, unless you mess up completely, the meat will always be moist. A young duck is what you want, as old ducks tend to get tough. The feet and legs are the best indicators of age: when they are young, the feet bend easily; with more use they become tough and gnarled. The only other thing you need to look for in a duck is as plump a breast as you can find.

PARTRIDGE (*see* recipes, pages 130–133) Related to the pheasant, the partridge is available in two types: the English grey and the French red-legged. Even the French confess to the grey having the best flavour.

Young birds are the best, and these have bendy beaks and pointed wing-tip feathers (the latter become round with age). If you want your young bird to remain moist, I suggest stuffing its cavity with butter and herbs.

PHEASANT (*see* recipes, pages 126–129) This is very attractive long-tailed game bird, originally Asian, but now very happily living in Europe. The pheasant cock is a bigger bird and more colourful than a hen. Many connoisseurs say the hen has more flavour, and it definitely has a bigger breast than a cock. However, if you are throwing a dinner party, a hen will feed two people, but three people can feast on a cock at a push.

VEGETABLES

AUBERGINE A lot of thought went into whether I should add the Mediterranean aubergine to a list of seasonal British ingredients. But I do grow and sell, albeit under glass, the most amazing purple Violetti aubergines, so I decided to include them here.

Nearly all aubergines on sale are black, shiny and pear shaped, and none of these should need salting. There are long, thinner varieties, known as Cyprus aubergines, that have a slightly sweeter taste. You may be lucky enough to get a white one but I doubt it. For the best aubergine experience I strongly suggest you check out the purple Violetti.

BEETROOT (*see* recipes, pages 146–149) Beetroot got off to a bad start for me and I'm sure most people my age have awful memories of little round beetroots stored in jars of vinegar.

Most of the beetroot you buy, raw or cooked, will be large and round. You can find baby beets, and these are sweeter and softer. There are now golden varieties which, even when cooked, retain their deep yellow gold. If you cut a variety named Chioggia in half, you will see a white spiral running through the deep purple. My favourite beetroot, though, is the Cheltenham, which is shaped very much like a parsnip: no matter how big this beetroot gets, the flesh inside remains wonderfully soft.

BOK-CHOI (*see* page 72)

BORLOTTI BEAN In its natural state, the borlotti is one of the most beautiful vegetables in the world. It has a bright red pod with white marbling. Even the beans inside are pretty: white with black marbling. Unfortunately, when you cook them they turn brown.

CALABRESE (*see also* Sprouting broccoli, page 27, and recipes, pages 54–55) Calabrese is a brassica, which means it is a member of the cabbage family, along with cauliflowers. In fact, calabrese and cauliflower are amazingly similar. Those florets you see on both vegetables are actually immature flower buds that refuse to develop any further.

Calabrese, botanically speaking, is a very new member of the vegetable kingdom, and the name comes from Calabria in southern Italy where it was first bred. I much prefer sprouting broccoli.

CANNELLINI BEAN I include cannellini beans in this list because I've managed to grow them myself. The bean itself is completely white and kidney shaped. The pods are a bright canary yellow, and if fading to white the beans are old. If the pod ends are very soft then the cannellini is past its prime.

CARDOON A cardoon is a thistle of the same family as the globe artichoke, but it is the leafless stems that are eaten, not the flower. When harvested, they mostly resemble a far wider and coarser Swiss chard. They should be firm and erect with no browning around the edges.

CARROT (*see* page 165 and recipes, pages 186–189; *see also* Baby Carrot, page 71, and recipes, pages 96–97)

CAULIFLOWER (*see* page 25)

CHILLI (*see* page 72)

COURGETTE (*see* page 73)

FENNEL There are a few types of fennel bulb, but they mostly fall into two categories: the longer flatter version, which is male, or the big, round, bulbous female 'Florence' fennel. The girlie variety is what you want. Its taste is sweeter and its skin is not as rough as the male variety.

Try to buy fennel with all its fern or fronds still intact. This deep green spidery leaf looks stunning scattered over the deep red of a tomato salad. It also has a much subtler flavour than the fennel flesh, which makes it virtually compulsory to stuff in a fish.

The flavour of fennel is unmistakably aniseed; a taste that I love. Sliced raw, fennel obviously keeps all its strong flavour, but this doesn't suit everyone. Roasted or braised in stock the flesh softens, as does the flavour. It can also be sliced lengthways, brushed with oil and griddled.

GLOBE ARTICHOKE These rounded robust vegetables are actually the flower buds of a thistle. If they are left untouched on a plant they will produce the most beautiful spiky flowers.

Many artichokes have long spikes attached to their outer leaves and I've often impaled a finger on these. There are two ways of dealing with them. Either cut off the top third, then peel away and discard the outer leaves until you are left with a circular frisbee-type base containing the triangular, hairy choke. Then all you do is remove the choke and eat the base or heart. Alternatively, boil it whole. This way you can prise the flesh contained within the broad leaves out with your teeth. Just remember to remove that hairy choke when you get down to the base. A gentler introduction to the artichoke is to cook a baby one. These haven't yet formed a hairy choke inside and can be cooked whole or halved.

There are two things to remember. The first is never to lick your fingers while, or after, handling artichokes, as it tastes absolutely disgusting. The second is that eating an artichoke will unpleasantly alter the taste of any wine you drink alongside it.

HORSERADISH The name is derived from the fierce heat of the root, which can make your throat hot and sore, or hoarse. It is also hell to prepare, with a tough skin that takes some peeling. This can make your eyes water much worse than onions or mustard could ever hope to. We all know that horseradish is a beautiful accompaniment to roast beef, but it also matches up very well with beetroot and offal.

LEEK (*see* page 165 and recipes, pages 196–199)

MARROW Hardly anybody seems to eat marrows nowadays. I think maybe the size puts people off, but a marrow is really just a big fat courgette. You can cut chunks off and roast, par-boil or fry them. My favourite way is to stuff a marrow with mince and bake it.

MUSHROOMS (*see* page 26)

ONIONS (*see* page 26)

POTATOES (*see* page 166 and recipes, pages 182–185; *see also* New and salad potatoes, page 26 and recipes, pages 60–63)

RUNNER BEANS (*see* page 74)

SALSIFY This is, at first appearance, a dirty brown stick, but its skin, although rough, comes away easily with peeling. The inside is a creamy greyish off-white and must be placed into acidulated water immediately as it will discolour. Once peeled and chopped, it is best served roasted. For me, its taste is creamy and earthy at the same time, with an almost nutty after-taste.

SHALLOTS (*see* page 27)

SPINACH (*see* page 27)

SWEETCORN (*see* recipes, pages 142–145)
Sweetcorn is a type of maize, which is a type of grass, and one of the most important food crops in the world.

Nobody else in Europe eats their corn on the cob as we do. I think corn-cob eating is one of the more acceptable imports from our North American cousins. One whinge – those silly little prissy forks that are sold to hold your corn cobs. You don't need forks; what you need is a big napkin to wipe your hands and chin afterwards. One lady did suggest to me that those forks were very practical and stopped you burning your fingers. I did point out to her that if the corn cob was too hot for your fingers, then it would be far too hot for your mouth too!

SWISS CHARD (*see* page 74 and *see* recipes, pages 86–89)

FRUIT

APPLE (*see* recipes, pages 150–153) British apple orchards, although now fast disappearing, pre-date the Roman invasion. Sadly, most of the apples available in our shops now are foreign imports, which are having a catastrophic effect on our ancient orchards. Over the last 15 years, nearly 60 per cent of independent apple-growers in the UK have disappeared.

The amazing variety in shape, size, colour, texture and flavour makes the apple a very regional, specialist foodstuff. Each of us should enjoy and celebrate the apples particular to our area. Unfortunately most of the population now shop in supermarkets and this is a very bad thing for English apples. Supermarkets desire – indeed insist on – complete uniformity, not just in individual stores, but throughout their entire network. This, of course, means that only the very biggest of orchards can possibly supply the whole country, leading to the death of the regional apple-grower. This is why our supermarket shelves are stacked high with foreign imports of Granny Smith and Golden Delicious.

Of course the best way to sample an apple is to wait until it ripens on a tree and pick it yourself, which is unlikely to happen, I know! Virtually all the apples we sample have been kept in storage, and any apple's crispness and flavour will deteriorate with storage. Apple-picking begins around August and ends in October, and apples stored in autumn are still fine just after Christmas. I refuse to eat an apple after January, but apples are on sale to us twelve months of the year. How is this possible? These apples will definitely have been refrigerated, which murders the flavour of any fruit, as fruit hates the cold. But I fear there are worse practices than big refrigerators. Many apples undergoing long storage must have been picked far, far from ripe; the riper the fruit, the quicker it will deteriorate. I have a deep suspicion that many fruits available to us well out of season must have undergone some sort of gas flushing.

The point I'm trying to make is that you can be sure the smaller the orchard, the fresher and less stored and so therefore better tasting your apples will be. Look out for some of the following when on your travels: Ribston Pippin, Ashmeads Kernel (Yorkshire), Adams Pearmain (Norfolk), Falstaff, Limelight (Kent), Bens Red (Cornwall), Cox's Orange Pippin (Buckinghamshire), Discovery, Flame (Essex), Lord Lambourne (Bedfordshire), Cheddar Cross (Bristol), Duke of Devonshire (Cumbria), Elmore Pippin (Gloucestershire), Marriage Maker (Leicestershire), Lord Burghley (Northamptonshire), John Standish (Berkshire), Harry Pring (Surrey), Bakers Delicious (Wales) and Irish Peach (Ireland).

BLACKBERRY (see recipes, pages 158–161)
I have mixed emotions when I see blackberries. I'm happy that they've arrived; lovely plump little things, sweet, yet tart at the same time. But I also get a little sad. Blackberries are the last of the soft fruit to show, so when you see the first of the blackberries, it's the beginning of the end of the soft fruit season.

MEDLAR Not many of us ever get to try a medlar,
because there are few in cultivation, and even the wild ones seem to be disappearing. It is a small, yellow-brown, pear-shaped fruit. Its flesh is grey when unripe and turns brown when ripe. The medlar has to over-ripen in order to be good, and I mean nearly rotten. This over-ripening is called 'bletting'. In this state, the medlar has a deep, mildly acidic flavour, not unlike red wine.

PEAR (see page 166 and see recipes, pages 200–203)

PLUMS (see recipes, pages 154–157) When
buying, look for plump fruits with tight unwrinkled skins. The good news is that plums will continue to ripen at home. Most imported and refrigerated plums won't ripen very well, but a home-grown, unripe but unrefrigerated fruit will soften up nicely.

Plums are, of course, very fine when cooked. They make an excellent compote to be served with game, pork or even your Christmas turkey, and plums are fantastic jammers. Their high pectin level means they don't have to be cooked for as long as other fruits. Dried, of course, they become prunes.

I will list for you now a few varieties that I think you should take the trouble to source. Before I do,

I just want to moan a bit more. The Victoria plum seems hugely popular. It has neither good texture nor deep flavour. The reason it's so well known is that it is the most prolific fruiter of the last 200 years. The fact that it grows so well does not mean that it eats very well. Instead, look out for: greengages, Marjorie Seedling, Burbank, Kirkes Blue and Yellow Egg. And, although you're unlikely to encounter it, I have at Secretts Farm a fruit to rival any other. This little beauty is an opal plum. It has a purple-blue skin over which a white fuzzy haze forms like a mist. The flesh inside is deep orange and tastes like the finest of peaches...

QUINCE The quince is a big, hard, yellow fruit
that can be apple- or pear-shaped. In fact, the quince is the same family as the apple and the pear but, unlike its cousins, it cannot be eaten without cooking. An important quality in the quince is the huge pectin level in its seeds, which is why quince features in many jams, jellies and marmalades. When cooked, it gives off a wonderful scent. When cooked alongside other fruit, it colours the whole a very pretty pink.

SALADS

RADICCHIO A little round red ball of a salad
head, radicchio is actually a member of the chicory family and tastes like it, being rather bitter. It's the colour that is so impressive: deep ruby red, soft leaves, with white veins running through them. Never use the thick stalky bit. Chewing on thick bitter stalk is not an enjoyable experience. This bitter leaf benefits from a sweet dressing.

ROCKET (see page 76 and see recipes, pages 98–101)

WATERCRESS I simply adore these hot peppery
leaves, but I've always hated handling them. They are picked and packed tightly in polystyrene boxes along with a bucket of ice and a loose-fitting lid. This means, in the heat of packing up restaurant vegetable orders, that you regularly douse yourself down with ice-cold water. Fantastic in the early hours of a freezing January morning!

Watercress is a member of the mustard family and it is from the mustard lineage that it gets its heat. What with watercress having been with us for centuries, I can't understand the current popularity of rocket. A direct comparison will find watercress to be a softer, prettier, and much more flavoursome salad item.

Watercress leaves should be a dark vivid green and its one downside is that it has the shelf life of a snowball. I still think it is unrivalled as a salad item, and it makes wonderful soups served hot or cold.

HERBS

MINT I simply adore the smell and taste of mint, and it's definitely my favourite herb. My grandmother grew mint in her garden and I would help her pick it, then watch her chop it up with white wine vinegar for mint sauce to go with her roast lamb. I always chuck a sprig into a pot of new potatoes boiling away. I also like it in with peas, although many people will disagree. Chopped and mixed with Greek yoghurt it makes a fine dressing or dip, but it also works wonders chopped and tossed through a salad.

Most of the mint we use is the 'spear' variety. Peppermint has a stronger flavour, but now you can, if you look hard enough, get your hands on 'apple' or 'pineapple' mint. These are subtly flavoured with the fruit of their name but feel rather hairy in comparison to spearmint.

ROSEMARY I think cooks underestimate the powerful flavour of rosemary more than any other herb. Rosemary is a very woody herb, which means it should go in at the beginning of your dish. Either remove the leaves and chop them well, or add a whole sprig, to be removed before serving.

Rosemary is perfect as a flavouring for lamb, pork, veal or chicken. You can also sprinkle it over a tray of vegetables that you would like to roast.

SAGE This is a member of the mint family, with a woody stem and thick leaves. This means that sage should always be added when you begin to cook a dish. We know it from childhood in sage and onion stuffing. I believe sage is the herb of big dishes. It's perfect with pork or chicken. You can use it whenever you cook fatty meats, and it's an absolute star with offal. I make no secret of my passion for the foods of Italy, and there it's fried in butter in a sauce for pasta, used in the famous saltimbocca, or added to tomatoes cooked with garlic and oil.

THYME Thyme's fragrance is warm and earthy. It comes with grey-green bud-type leaves, sometimes just grey, sometimes green.

Thyme is one part of the holy trinity with bay leaf and parsley that makes up a bouquet garni. Being a strong woody herb, it should always be used at the beginning of your dish. Either pull the leaves from the stem and chop them well or use a large sprig that you can remove from the pot before serving.

Thyme is perfect for a stuffing, casseroles, chicken, fish, game, or added to tomatoes. Lemon thyme is now available, but why bother with this? Use normal thyme in your dish and add a squeeze of lemon at the end.

NUTS

CHESTNUT I have fond memories of eating roasted chestnuts when coming home with my grandfather after watching Millwall play football.

Chestnuts can, of course, be ground into flour for baking, or included in stews or purées, but the roasted nuts are what still turn me on. They're easy to prepare. Make sure you put a cross in the shell first before putting them in the oven, otherwise they will explode. When the nut is soft and the shell is black, put them in a clear plastic bag and rub them vigorously between your hands. Amazingly, all the shells will come off.

HAZELNUT (*see* page 167)

WALNUT Walnuts are wonderful tossed through salads and they go very well with chicken, or in the stuffing thereof. At the start of the season, you can get very fresh nuts, moist to the touch, and milky in flavour. These are called 'wet walnuts'. My favourite breakfast is still walnuts and yoghurt drizzled with some honey.

Duck

(*see also* page 117) A duck has rich, succulent meat. Unfortunately, there is never enough meat on one duck for two people and always too much for one. The most famous varieties of eating duck are Aylesbury, Gressingham, Nantes and Barbary.

When cooking a duck breast, there is no need to put any oil in the pan. Just get the pan very hot and put the breast in fat-side down. That fat will render, giving you enough liquid to cook the meat on the other side. If roasting a whole duck, pierce the skin all over and let the fat drip into the tray. Empty the tray every 15 minutes.

Duck breasts with red wine sauce

I can't resist a duck, it's as simple as that. Be careful when browning; the duck is a very fatty bird, and I still bear the scar on my right hand from a volcano-like eruption of hot fat from the pan when browning duck.

4 duck breasts, about 250–300g (9–10½ oz) each
125ml (4fl oz) beef stock
125ml (4fl oz) red wine
1 tsp sun-dried tomato purée
salt and pepper
a squeeze of lemon juice
20g (¾ oz) butter, cold and cubed

MARINADE
5 garlic cloves, peeled and crushed
2 tbsp balsamic vinegar
2 tbsp chopped rosemary leaves

Serves 4

Combine the marinade ingredients together. Using a sharp knife, score lines in the fat of the duck breasts. Spread the marinade over the duck breasts. Put them in the refrigerator for 30 minutes, covered.

Preheat the oven to 190°C/375°F/Gas 5.

Heat a large frying pan over a medium heat. Add the duck breasts, skin-side down, with any remaining marinade and cook for about 6 minutes. Turn and cook for another 6 minutes. Remove the duck from the pan and transfer to the oven. Cook for a further 5 minutes, then rest in a warm place.

Spoon off any excess fat from the pan. Add the stock and wine, and bring to the boil. Cook over a high heat until the liquid has reduced by half. Whisk in the tomato purée, season and add just a trickle of lemon juice to taste. Remove from the heat, add the butter and swirl the pan to thicken the sauce.

Slice the breasts and arrange them on warm plates. Spoon over the sauce and serve at once.

Duckling with green peas

Oh yes! I don't know which I prefer, the duckling or the peas – a marriage made in heaven.

1 duckling, about 2–2.5kg (4½–5lb)
salt and pepper
40g (1½oz) butter
15 small shallots, peeled
55g (2oz) smoked streaky bacon, cut into thin strips

500g (18oz) frozen peas
2 tbsp chopped chives
5 tbsp chicken stock

Serves 4

Preheat the oven to 220°C/425°F/Gas 7.

Wash and dry the duck. Prick the skin with a sharp skewer. Do not pierce the flesh. Season with salt and pepper. Place on a roasting rack over a roasting tin and roast for 40 minutes.

Melt the butter in a frying pan over a medium heat. Add the shallots and fry until lightly browned, about 8 minutes. Add the bacon and fry for a few minutes more. Add the peas, stir in the chives and remove from the heat.

Remove the duck from the oven. Spoon off any fat from the tin. Stir in the stock, then add the pea, shallot and bacon mixture. Return the duck on its rack to the tin and return to the oven for another 30 minutes, until cooked.

Serve the duck surrounded by the vegetables and juices.

Duck and chestnut casserole

The decision here is whether to serve this with mashed or roast potatoes. I still can't decide which is better.

1 duckling, about 2kg (4½lb), jointed into 8 pieces
salt and pepper
3 tbsp vegetable oil
175g (6oz) small shallots, peeled and halved
100g (3½oz) field mushrooms, sliced

300ml (10fl oz) red wine
300ml (10fl oz) beef stock
225g (8oz) chestnuts, peeled
1 tsp cornflour

Serves 4

Preheat the oven to 180°C/350°F/Gas 4.

Season the duck pieces. Heat the oil in a large frying pan over a medium heat and brown the duck pieces, about 4 minutes each. Remove the duck from the pan.

Add the shallots to the pan and fry for about 10 minutes, until well browned. Add the mushrooms to the pan and cook for a couple of minutes. Now add the red wine to the pan and boil to reduce by half.

Pour the contents of the pan into a casserole, and stir in the stock. Add the duck and chestnuts, and season with salt and pepper. Bake for 1½ hours with a lid on.

Remove the duck pieces and skim off any excess fat. Mix the cornflour with a little of the juices, then stir into the sauce and cook for 4–5 minutes. Pour over the duck and serve immediately.

Pheasant

(*see also* page 117) Pheasant is best roasted or casseroled. Like all game, it does tend towards being dry, so a jacket of fatty bacon with butter smeared underneath is a good bet, as is basting regularly. You may want to cook the breast and legs separately, as the breast is tender, but the legs have far more sinew.

Pheasant with apples

I think the sharp sweetness of the apple matches terrifically well with the strong meat of the pheasant.

1 fat pheasant
salt and pepper
15g (½oz) plain flour, plus extra for dusting
85g (3oz) butter
1 large onion, peeled and finely chopped
2 celery stalks, chopped
2 eating apples, peeled, cored and sliced

250ml (9fl oz) chicken stock
250ml (9fl oz) dry cider
1 bouquet garni (parsley, thyme and bay leaf)
4 tbsp crème fraîche

Serves 2

Preheat the oven to 180°C/350°F/Gas 4.

Wash the bird and dry with kitchen paper. Season all over with salt and pepper and dust with a little flour.

Melt 55g (2oz) of the butter in a large flameproof casserole over a medium heat. Fry the bird until light brown all over, then remove from the casserole. Put in the onion and fry very gently for about 5 minutes.

Add the celery and half of the apples, and sweat for another 2 minutes. Now add the 15g (½oz) flour, and stir until well mixed in. Very gradually add the stock and cider, stirring all the time to make a smooth sauce. When it comes to the boil, return the bird to the casserole, add the bouquet garni, cover, and braise in the oven for about 40 minutes, until cooked through.

Melt the remaining butter in a frying pan over a medium heat. Add the remaining apple and fry gently until golden brown, about 10 minutes. Keep the pan aside and reheat just before serving.

Remove the casserole from the oven, and place the bird on a serving dish. Strain the sauce through a sieve into a small pan. Bring to the boil and simmer for a few minutes, until quite thick. Stir in the crème fraîche and heat up. Check the seasoning before serving with the pheasant and buttered apples.

Pheasant in whisky sauce

Pheasant is one of the larger game birds and, thankfully, not as fiddly as some. The sauce is the real winner here, deep and rich in colour and flavour.

2 pheasants
salt and pepper
a little plain flour, for dusting
55g (2oz) butter
100g (3½oz) streaky bacon, diced

100ml (3½fl oz) whisky
175ml (6fl oz) white wine
4 tbsp crème fraîche

Serves 4

Wash the birds and dry on kitchen paper. Season all over with salt and pepper and dust with a little flour.

Over a medium heat, melt the butter in a lidded pan or casserole which will just fit the two birds. Add the bacon and cook until just browned. Remove the bacon from the pot. Now brown the birds all over. Return the bacon to the pot and place the birds on top, breast-side down. Add the whisky and let it bubble for a few seconds. Cover the pot and leave to simmer gently for 20 minutes. Turn the birds over to breast-side up and add the wine. Bring to the boil and cover again. Cook for another 20 minutes, simmering gently. Check they are cooked through.

Remove the cooked birds to a serving dish, carve them up and keep warm. Add the crème fraîche to the liquid in the pan, bring to the boil and simmer until the sauce is quite thick. Check the seasoning and serve with the pheasant.

Pheasant braised with mushrooms

There are lots of flavours in this recipe, but I think it's the redcurrant jelly, stirred into the sauce at the end, that really completes the dish for me. Everybody should have a go at cooking pheasant during the season. This dish is a great place to start.

2 pheasants, breasts and leg portions removed
salt and pepper
a little plain flour, for dusting
20g (¾ oz) butter
1 tbsp vegetable oil
8 small shallots, peeled
200g (7oz) field mushrooms, sliced
1 tsp thyme leaves

250ml (9fl oz) red wine
250ml (9fl oz) chicken or vegetable stock
1 tbsp cornflour
2 tbsp dark soy sauce
2 tbsp redcurrant jelly
2 bay leaves

Serves 6

Preheat the oven to 180°C/350°F/Gas 4.

Discard the carcasses (unless you want to make stocks with them). Season the meat all over with salt and pepper and dust with a little flour.

Melt the butter and oil in a large frying pan over a medium heat. Add the whole shallots and some of the pheasant portions, browning the meat all over. Remove the browned meat to a medium casserole. Repeat with the rest of the meat. As the shallots become browned all over, add to the meat in the casserole.

Add the mushrooms and thyme to the pan and cook for 2 minutes, stirring often. Transfer to the casserole.

Add the wine and stock to the pan and bring to the boil. Blend the cornflour with the soy sauce, and add to the liquid, stirring all the time. Add the redcurrant jelly and the bay leaves. Pour the sauce over the meat and cover the casserole.

Braise in the oven for about 1½ hours, until the meat is tender.

Partridge

(see also page 117) Partridges are small birds, perfectly sized for a single portion. They have a pale flesh, almost like chicken, but don't hang for too long, four days at most.

Partridge casserole

It does take a while to cook this one but it's well worth it, and of course you have got vegetables to serve with your bird at the end.

2 partridges
2 shallots, peeled
2 rashers streaky bacon
salt and pepper
2 onions, peeled and sliced
350g (12oz) carrots, peeled and sliced
60g (2¼oz) back bacon, diced

2 bay leaves
15g (½oz) parsley leaves, chopped
1 tsp thyme leaves, chopped
1 Savoy cabbage, trimmed and quartered
900ml (1½ pints) chicken stock, hot

Serves 4

Preheat the oven to 170°C/325°F/Gas 3.

Put a whole shallot inside each bird. Lay a rasher of streaky bacon on the breasts of each bird. Season well.

Put the sliced onion and carrot, diced bacon and herbs in a large casserole. Season. Lay the birds on top.

Bring a large pan of salted water to the boil. Add the cabbage quarters and blanch for 3 minutes. Drain.

Arrange the cabbage quarters around the birds. Pour in the hot stock and bake, uncovered, for 2 hours.

Stuffed roast partridges

This is really easy to do. The stuffing gives the bird more flavour.

4 partridges
100g (3½oz) fresh white breadcrumbs
finely grated zest of 1 lemon
3 tbsp chopped parsley leaves
4 juniper berries, crushed in a pestle and mortar
1 tbsp raisins
2 tbsp finely chopped shallot

salt and pepper
1 medium egg, beaten
8 rashers streaky bacon, cut in half
55g (2oz) butter, melted

Serves 4

Preheat the oven to 180°C/350°F/Gas 4.

Wash the birds and dry with kitchen paper. Mix the breadcrumbs with the lemon zest, parsley, juniper berries, raisins and shallot. Season. Use the beaten egg to bind the stuffing. Stuff the birds with this mixture.

Tie the legs together with kitchen string. Season the birds, then cover the tops of the birds with half lengths of bacon. Brush with the melted butter.

Roast for 1 hour, until cooked through. Baste the birds a couple of times during cooking. Remove the string from the birds before serving.

Partridges in red wine

Cooking the birds in this way packs them full of flavour. The cooking liquid coats the birds completely and gives them a nice deep red colour.

2 partridges
1 onion, peeled and finely chopped
1 medium carrot, peeled and finely chopped
1 leek, white part only, cleaned and finely chopped
1 bouquet garni (1 celery stalk, 4 sprigs parsley,
  2 sprigs thyme and 1 small sprig sage)
450ml (16fl oz) chicken stock

3 anchovy fillets
55g (2oz) butter
450ml (16fl oz) red wine
salt and pepper

Serves 4

Wash the partridges and dry with kitchen paper. Mix all the vegetables together in a flameproof casserole with the bouquet garni. Pour in the stock, add the partridges and bring to the boil. Reduce to a simmer, cover, and cook gently on top of the stove for 1 hour, turning the birds halfway through the cooking time.

Using a pestle and mortar, pound the anchovies and half of the butter together. Add to the casserole after the hour's cooking. Also add the red wine and seasoning. Bring to the boil, reduce to a simmer, cover and cook gently for another hour, until the birds are very tender.

Transfer the birds to a warmed serving dish. Discard the bouquet garni and hard-boil the cooking liquid until very reduced and slightly thickened. When the sauce is the right consistency, stir in the remaining butter and adjust the seasoning.

Carve up the birds. Serve the sauce poured over the birds.

Cod (*see also* page 116 for information on sustainability) It's no wonder cod is Britain's favourite fish. Its meat is soft and comes off in large flakes. Fried, poached, cooked in pies, or mixed with potatoes to make fishcakes, it's perfect.

Cod fish pie

A very good pie, but this hasn't got mash over the top; it has slices of potatoes instead, a bit like a fishy hotpot.

500g (18oz) fillets of cod, skinned, in 3cm
(1¼ in) chunks
200g (7oz) smoked salmon, cut into strips
425g (15oz) large raw peeled prawns, black threads
removed (*see page 139*)
4 ripe tomatoes, skinned and chopped
salt and pepper
1.5kg (3lb 5oz) potatoes, peeled and sliced
30g (1¼ oz) butter

SAUCE
55g (2oz) butter
55g (2oz) plain flour
325ml (11fl oz) full-fat milk
150ml (5fl oz) dry vermouth
100ml (3½ fl oz) single cream
3 tbsp chopped dill leaves
1 tbsp lemon juice

Serves 6

For the sauce, place the butter, flour, milk and vermouth in a medium pan over a medium heat. Whisking all the time, bring to the boil and boil until the sauce is smooth and thick. Reduce the heat and simmer for 2 minutes. Season well and remove from the heat. Cover with clingfilm and leave to cool. When cool, stir in the cream, dill and lemon juice. Check the seasoning.

Preheat the oven to 200°C/400°F/Gas 6.

Mix together the fish, prawns and tomatoes with some seasoning. Put the mixture in a gratin dish. Pour the cooled sauce evenly over the fish/tomato mixture.

Bring a large pan of salted water to the boil. Add the sliced potatoes and cook for about 10 minutes. The potatoes should be just cooked but not falling apart. Drain and leave for a few minutes until cool enough to handle.

Arrange the potatoes over the sauced fish, overlapping the slices so it looks nice. Melt the butter and brush evenly over the potatoes. Season.

Bake for about 40 minutes, until the potatoes are golden.

Cod with a nut crust

I think this outside crust with bits of crunchy nut is different and yet sympathetic to the fish.

125g (4½oz) fresh brown breadcrumbs
55g (2oz) shelled walnuts, roughly chopped
3 tbsp chopped parsley leaves
3 tbsp chopped chives
finely grated zest of 1 lemon
freshly grated nutmeg

85g (3oz) butter
salt and pepper
4 fillets of cod, about 175–200g (6–7oz) each,
    scaled, skin left on
1 medium egg yolk, beaten

Serves 4

Preheat the oven to 200°C/400°F/Gas 6.

Put the breadcrumbs, walnuts, herbs, lemon zest and nutmeg in a bowl and mix together well. Melt the butter in a large frying pan over a medium-high heat. Stir in the crumb mixture and fry until the butter has been absorbed and the crumbs are starting to brown. Set aside.

Season the cod with salt and pepper, then put skin-side down on a baking tray. Brush the tops of the fish with the egg yolk, and press on the crumbs.

Bake for 15 minutes or so, until the flesh is flaky and the crumbs crisp.

Cod with parsley sauce

Everybody should learn how to make a white sauce. Once you've mastered it, you can then add all sorts of flavourings, such as the parsley here.

4 x 200g (7oz) fillets of cod, scaled, skin left on
a little plain flour, for dusting
30g (1¼ oz) butter

PARSLEY SAUCE
15g (½oz) butter
15g (½oz) plain flour

300ml (10fl oz) milk
2 tbsp crème fraîche
2 tbsp chopped parsley leaves
salt and pepper

Serves 4

Melt the butter for the parsley sauce in a small saucepan. Add the flour and stir for 2 minutes, then gradually add the milk, whisking all the time. When the sauce is thick, add the crème fraîche and parsley, and season well with salt and pepper. Leave to simmer very gently for 10 minutes, stirring occasionally.

Dust the skin-side of the cod fillets with a little flour. Melt the butter for the fish in a large frying pan over a medium heat. When the butter stops sizzling add the cod fillets, skin-side down. Cook for about 3 minutes, then very carefully turn each piece of fish over. Cook for about another 2 minutes. The cooking time will depend on the thickness of the fish.

Carefully, place each piece of fish skin-side down on a plate, and pour some parsley sauce over.

Prawns

(*see also* page 117) Marvellous things, prawns. Every public house in Britain should have bowls of the little pink beasties on the bar on Sunday lunchtimes free of charge. There are no huge prawns swimming around Britain. Australians have prawns big enough to use as boomerangs, but not over here. Ours are always little, and quite right. Our native chaps are known as the 'common prawn' and are always pink.

Prawns in beer batter

Let's face it, we all love a bit of fried food. Biting down through the batter to the plump prawns below is a real treat, and this recipe is so easy!

800g (1¾lb) shelled large prawns, uncooked
55g (2oz) plain flour
4 tbsp chopped dill
2 tbsp chopped parsley leaves
salt and pepper
vegetable oil, for deep-frying
lemon wedges, to serve

BATTER
150g (5½oz) plain flour
a pinch of salt
225ml (8fl oz) lager
30g (1¼oz) butter, melted
1 medium egg white

Serves 4

For the batter, sift the flour and salt into a large bowl. Make a well in the centre and pour in the lager. Whisk to a thick batter. Whisk in the melted butter, cover and leave to stand for an hour.

Preheat the oven to 150°C/300°F/Gas 2.

Using a small, sharp knife, make a very shallow cut all the way down the back of the prawns and remove the black line. This is the intestinal tract; you don't really want to eat that. Mix the flour with the chopped herbs and some seasoning.

Heat the oil in a large pan or wok to 190°C/375°F. Measure the temperature on a thermometer or, alternatively, drop a cube of bread into the oil: it should brown in about 30 seconds.

Meanwhile, whisk the egg white to stiff peaks and gently fold into the batter.

Dip each prawn into the flour-herb mix, then into the fluffy batter. Carefully drop into the hot oil. The prawns should be cooked in about 2 minutes, or when golden brown. Do not cook more than six or eight at a time. Remove from the oil and put on a baking sheet covered with kitchen paper and keep hot in the low oven while you cook the rest of the prawns.

Serve with lemon wedges.

Prawns with tarragon sauce

Discard your knife and fork, take this crustacean between your fingers, and dip. I think the slight aniseed flavour of tarragon is overlooked with shellfish. You decide.

12 large raw prawns in their shells
2 tbsp olive oil
300ml (10fl oz) dry white wine
2 garlic cloves, peeled and crushed
4 tbsp chopped parsley leaves
salt and pepper

TARRAGON SAUCE
4 tbsp chopped tarragon leaves
150ml (5fl oz) crème fraîche
1 tbsp mild mustard
a squeeze of lemon juice

Serves 4

To make the sauce, just mix together all the ingredients and season to taste.

Heat a large frying pan over a high heat. Brush the prawns with the oil. Add the prawns to the hot pan and cook for about 2 minutes, until pink. Add half of the wine with the garlic. Boil for 2 minutes, then add the parsley. Reduce the heat and add the rest of the wine, season and simmer for about 5 minutes.

Serve the prawns with the cooking juices poured over and a dollop of the sauce on the side.

Prawns with lettuce

You can serve this in a big bowl or pretty it up as a starter for a dinner party. Either way, I guarantee results.

55g (2oz) butter
2 cos lettuces, hearts only, shredded
1 tbsp finely chopped shallot
salt and pepper
150ml (5fl oz) double cream
2 tbsp chopped chives
500g (18oz) medium prawns, uncooked, shelled and
  black threads removed (*see* page 139)

a squeeze of lemon juice

CROÛTES
25g (1oz) butter
4 slices good bread, crusts removed

Serves 4

Melt the butter for the croûtes in a large frying pan over a medium heat and fry the slices of bread gently until crisp all over. Use more butter if needed. Remove the croûtes to kitchen paper and keep warm.

Melt the butter for the prawns in a large frying pan over a medium heat. Put in the shredded lettuce and shallot and turn in the butter until coated. Season with salt and pepper, cover the pan and cook for about 4 minutes.

Add the cream and chives to the pan and stir. Now add the prawns and a squeeze of lemon juice. Heat until the prawns are all pink and cooked through, about 3–4 minutes.

Pile each croûte with the prawn mixture and serve at once.

Sweetcorn

(*see also* page 119) I know I am considerably fortunate to work on a farm and have access to lip-smackingly fresh vegetables; all vegetables deteriorate as soon as you pick them, and you would not believe the speed with which sweetcorn deteriorates. My old mate and mentor, Charles Secrett, shares my passion for sweetcorn. If, as he recommends, you set up a camping stove next to a corn plant and cook a cob as soon as you pick it, you will be amazed. I'm not suggesting you never buy a corn cob from a shop again, but if you do get the chance to cook one as fresh as this, please do. In fact, call me and we'll set up a cob party at Charles' farm.

Corn pudding

The Tabasco and Worcestershire sauces liven up this little pudding. It's great, especially served with any roast poultry, but it is very filling.

3 corn cobs
30g (1¼ oz) butter
5 rashers streaky bacon, cut into little strips
450g (1lb) leeks, cleaned and shredded
1 red pepper, seeded and diced
salt and pepper
2 tbsp chopped parsley leaves

3 medium egg yolks
1 tsp English mustard
600ml (1 pint) double cream
6 drops Tabasco sauce
1 tsp Worcestershire sauce

Serves 6

Preheat the oven to 180°C/350°F/Gas 4.

Bring a large pan of water to the boil. Drop in the corn cobs, and blanch for 4 minutes. Drain. When cool enough to handle, cut off the corn kernels with a sharp knife.

Melt the butter in a large frying pan over a medium heat. Add the bacon and fry until crisp. Add the leek and red pepper and fry until all the liquid has evaporated. Season. Stir in the corn and parsley, then put the bacon-vegetable mixture into a gratin dish.

In a large bowl, whisk together the egg yolks, mustard, cream and both of the sauces. Pour the mixture over the vegetables and bake for about 45 minutes, until just set and golden. Leave to sit for 10 minutes before serving.

Corn cakes with salsa

These are just fun. The amount of chilli you add to your salsa is up to you.

3 large corn cobs, kernels sliced off
1 red onion, peeled and chopped
2 medium eggs
15g (½oz) chopped parsley leaves
125g (4½oz) plain flour
1 tsp baking powder
salt and pepper
vegetable oil, for shallow-frying

SALSA
1 ripe avocado, peeled and diced

15g (½oz) chopped parsley leaves
2 ripe tomatoes, chopped
2 tbsp lemon juice
2 tbsp olive oil
2 tbsp spring onions, finely sliced
2 red chillies, seeded and finely sliced (or how you prefer)

Serves 4–6

Preheat the oven to its lowest setting.

Place two-thirds of the corn in a food processor with the onion, eggs, parsley, flour, baking powder, and salt and pepper. Whizz until well mixed. Turn out into a bowl and stir in the remaining corn.

For the salsa, just mix together the ingredients and stir gently to combine.

Heat a little oil in a large frying pan over a medium-high heat. When hot, drop in 2 tbsp of the corn mixture per cake. Cook for 1 minute each side. Put the cooked cakes on a baking tray covered with kitchen paper and keep warm in the oven while you continue making the rest of the cakes.

When all the cakes are done, serve the hot cakes with the salsa.

Beetroot

(see also page 117) I must confess I didn't go anywhere near a beetroot for years. It was the ladies at the River Café who changed my point of view. It was there that I first sampled roast beetroots served with creamed horseradish.

If you can, try to buy your beets with the root and leaves attached. Here you have three vegetables for the price of one. The stems are delicious and crunchy and the leaves, cooked gently, are like spinach.

Roast beetroot and chestnuts

It's nice to have a bit of crunch with your beetroot. The sprinkle of parsley at the end really makes a difference: the vibrant green specks against the deep beetroot purple give this dish visual flair.

750g (1lb 10oz) raw beetroots, peeled and cut into
   4cm (1½in) chunks
4 rashers streaky bacon, diced
3 tbsp olive oil
3 tbsp balsamic vinegar

1 tsp caster sugar
salt and pepper
1 x 200g (7oz) packet peeled whole chestnuts
2 tbsp chopped parsley leaves

Serves 4–6

Preheat the oven to 200°C/400°F/Gas 6.

Place the beetroot chunks in a large baking tray. Mix together the bacon, oil, vinegar, sugar and a little seasoning. Pour over the beets, and stir.

Bake for 1½ hours. Stir a couple of times during cooking.

Stir in the chestnuts, and return to the oven for a further 15 minutes. Sprinkle over the parsley just before serving.

Beetroot crumble

This goes well with oily fish, and also sits very happily with roast meats.

500g (18oz) raw beetroots, washed well
70g (2½ oz) butter
55g (2oz) plain flour
450ml (16fl oz) milk
3 tbsp crème fraîche
3 tbsp horseradish sauce

salt and pepper
75g (2¾ oz) fresh white breadcrumbs
3 tbsp finely grated Parmesan
2 tbsp rolled oats

Serves 4–6

Preheat the oven to 180°C/350°F/Gas 4 and bake the beets as described in paragraph 2 of the method for Beetroot Relish below, but for just 1½ hours. Remove from the oven and allow to cool. Peel off and discard the foil and skins. Chop into quite large bits. Place in an ovenproof dish, and increase the oven temperature to 200°C/400°F/Gas 6.

Melt 55g (2oz) of the butter in a small pan. Sprinkle in the flour and cook for 2 minutes. Stirring all the time, pour in the milk gradually until the sauce is smooth and thick. Simmer very gently for 5 minutes, stirring occasionally. Stir in the crème fraîche and horseradish, and season well. Pour the sauce over the beets.

Mix the breadcrumbs, Parmesan and oats together with a little salt and pepper. Sprinkle evenly over the sauced beets. Dot the remaining butter over the top evenly. Bake for 30 minutes, until golden brown.

Beetroot relish

This is a fearsome beast and no mistake. Get some indication of the flavour by sniffing the pan as it's stewing.

500g (18oz) raw beetroots, washed well
1 red onion, peeled and thinly sliced
2 cooking apples, peeled, cored and sliced
125ml (4fl oz) red wine vinegar
125ml (4fl oz) malt vinegar

5 tbsp horseradish sauce
55g (2oz) light brown sugar
55g (2oz) raisins

Makes about 1kg (2¼lb)

Preheat the oven to 180°C/350°F/Gas 4.

Trim the beet stalks to about 2cm (¾in) long. Wrap each beet in foil and bake, until soft when pierced with a fine skewer. This should take about 2 hours. Remove from the oven and allow to cool. Peel off and discard the foil and the beetroot skins.

In the meantime, put the onion and apple in a medium pan with the vinegars. Bring to the boil, reduce to a simmer and cook for about 20 minutes, until the onion is soft.

Dice the beets and add to the pan with the rest of the ingredients. Heat gently until the sugar has dissolved. Raise the heat to a simmer and cook for another 10 minutes until the relish is thick.

Pour the relish into warm, sterilized jars (*see* page 65). Seal with wax discs and cellophane covers. Leave in a cool, dark place for 6 weeks before using.

Apples

(see also page 119) The apple is a cornerstone of our rich food heritage. Can you imagine a world without apple crumble, apple tarts, baked apple or apple chutney? I know I can't. Personally, I think any Englishman saying 'no' to apple crumble should have his citizenship revoked.

Baked apple dumplings

Dig beneath the pastry of these lovely dumplings and get at the gorgeous squishy apple below.

4 cooking apples, peeled
55g (2oz) dark brown sugar
½ tsp vanilla essence
1 tbsp double cream
1 medium egg white
milk, for brushing

1 tbsp caster sugar
a pinch of salt
175g (6oz) butter, cold and cubed
2–3 tbsp cold water

Serves 4

PASTRY
275g (9½oz) plain flour

For the pastry, in a food processor, whizz the flour, sugar, salt and butter until the mixture looks like breadcrumbs. Slowly add cold water, a teaspoon at a time, until the mixture forms a dough and is the right texture. Remove from the machine and knead the dough lightly, until smooth. Cover with clingfilm and chill for 10 minutes.

Preheat the oven to 220°C/425°F/Gas 7.

Using a sharp, small knife, core the apples from the stem end without cutting through to the base. Mix the sugar with the vanilla essence and cream in a small bowl. Fill the cores of the apples with the mixture.

Roll out half the dough on a floured surface. Cut out two circles with a 15cm (6in) saucer and two smaller circles with a 10cm (4in) cutter. Brush the larger rounds with egg white. Place an apple on each round. Top the apple with a smaller round. Mould the top bit of pastry around the apple, and brush the edges with water. Now bring up the lower bit and mould around and over the top one. Squeeze gently to seal. Place the covered apples on a baking sheet, making sure not to make any holes in them. Repeat the procedure with the rest of the apples.

If you have any pastry left and you feel like it, make some leaf decorations and stick them on to the apples with water. Brush the pastry with some milk and bake for 30 minutes.

Reduce the oven temperature to 180°C/350°F/Gas 4 and bake for another 20 minutes.

Apple pie

This is a very good apple pie. The mixed spice makes a difference here, as do the ground almonds. Custard, cream or ice-cream to serve? Your choice!

PASTRY
225g (8oz) plain flour
55g (2oz) self-raising flour
25g (1oz) caster sugar, plus extra for dredging
a pinch of salt
175g (6oz) butter, cold and cubed
1 medium egg, beaten with 2 tbsp cold water
milk, for brushing

FILLING
25g (1oz) plain flour

300g (10½oz) caster sugar
1 tsp ground mixed spice
finely grated zest of 1 lemon
1kg (2¼ lb) cooking apples, peeled, cored and sliced
25g (1oz) ground almonds
25g (1oz) butter, cold and diced
8 cloves
1 tbsp lemon juice

Serves 6

For the pastry, whizz the flours, sugar, salt and butter in a food processor until the mixture looks like breadcrumbs. Slowly add enough of the egg mixture until a dough is formed. Remove from the machine and knead the dough lightly, until smooth. Cover with clingfilm and chill for 30 minutes.

Preheat the oven to 220°C/425°F/Gas 7.

For the filling, mix the flour, caster sugar, spice and lemon zest together. Add the sliced apples and mix well.

Roll out just over half the dough on a floured surface and use to line a 25cm (10in) flan tin or large pie plate. Sprinkle the ground almonds evenly over the pastry. Top with half the apple mix. Add half the diced butter and 4 cloves. Top with the remaining apples. Dot with the remaining butter and cloves. Sprinkle over the lemon juice along with any apple juices.

Roll out the rest of the pastry on a floured surface. Brush the edges of the pastry in the tin or pie plate with water. Cover with the rolled-out pastry, squeezing the edges together really well to seal. Trim the excess pastry with a knife angled outwards. Neaten the edges if necessary. If you want, use the remaining pastry to make leaves for decoration. Brush the leaves with water and stick on to the pie. Cut two small neat holes in the middle of the pie.

Brush the pie with a little milk and bake for 30 minutes. Reduce the oven temperature to 190°C/375°F/Gas 5. Bake for another 30 minutes, until the pastry is golden brown. If the pie is browning too fast, just cover loosely with a sheet of foil.

As soon as the pie is cooked, remove from the oven and dredge with extra caster sugar. The pie is best served at room temperature.

Plums

(see also page 120) The plum comes in many colours and sizes. A properly ripe plum is a delight. With soft, deep-flavoured flesh, it will give you a sensation of a fresh fruit drink and the richness of a good Burgundy.

It's not much loved nowadays, the poor plum. As stone fruits go, I suppose they're quite hard work. I think they've suffered from the importation of peaches and nectarines. The plum's flesh is, I have to confess, firmer, and its skin is not as soft. Much of the problem, I feel, lies in the poor quality of the imported plum. Some of the fruits I've sampled, flown in from South America, would make jolly good cricket balls. If these imported plums have been a child's first experience, it is no wonder that plums are declining in popularity.

Plum jam

I'm a big jammer me, and the plum is relatively easy. It reaches its setting point faster than most fruits.

1.25kg (2¾ lb) plums, halved and stoned
300ml (10fl oz) water
1kg (2¼ lb) preserving sugar

Makes approx. 2 kg (4½ lb)

Preheat the oven to its lowest setting, and sterilize the jars (*see* page 65).

Put the plums and water in a preserving pan. Bring to the boil, then simmer for about 30 minutes, until the fruit is really soft. Gradually stir in the sugar, stirring all the time, until it is fully dissolved.

Bring the jam to the boil again and boil hard to setting point. This should take about 15 minutes. On a sugar thermometer this is 105°C/221°F. If you wish to test whether the jam is ready, put a saucer in the freezer in advance. When you think the jam is ready, take the pan off the heat and put a teaspoon of jam on the cold saucer. When the jam is cool, run a finger through it and if it wrinkles, it is ready.

Pot into the warm sterilized jars. Cover each with a disc of waxed paper. When cool, cover with cellophane covers and the lids, if you have any. This jam is best left for a month before eating.

Plum tart

This tastes every bit as good as it looks. If I were you, I would make two tarts, as one will disappear in minutes. Very good made with greengages.

1 packet ready-rolled puff pastry

FILLING
100g (3½oz) ground almonds
70g (2½oz) butter, softened
100g (3½oz) caster sugar
1 medium egg

1 medium egg white
500g (18oz) plums, halved and stoned
55g (2oz) soft brown sugar
½ tsp ground cinnamon

Serves 6

Preheat the oven to 220°C/425°F/Gas 7.

In a food processor, work the almonds, butter and caster sugar until well mixed. Add the egg and egg white and whizz to a smooth cream.

Unroll the pastry on to a large baking sheet. Tidy up the edges with a sharp knife, if needed. Using a sharp knife, lightly cut a line 3cm (1¼in) from the edges all around, making sure you do not cut all the way through.

Spread the almond mixture carefully all over the pastry, inside the cut lines. Now place the plum halves, cut-side up, all over the almond mix, again within the lines. Mix the soft brown sugar with the cinnamon and sprinkle all over the plums.

Bake for about 30 minutes, until puffed up and golden. Serve warm with cream.

Plums in port

Plums are not everybody's favourite stone fruit. I think they would be if they were poached like this and then served with a reduced liquor. The sauce is rich and deep and truly delicious.

750ml (26fl oz) water
250g (9oz) granulated sugar
150ml (5fl oz) port
1kg (2¼ lb) plums

Serves 4

Put the water and sugar in a large pan and slowly bring to the boil, stirring until the sugar dissolves. Boil, without stirring for about 5 minutes. Add the port and the plums and bring to a gentle simmer. Poach the plums for about 5 minutes until they are soft but not falling apart.

Carefully remove the plums from the liquid. Boil the liquid until it is well reduced and syrupy. Pour the syrup over the plums and chill. Serve with crème fraîche and crisp biscuits.

Blackberries

(see also page 120) Blackberries are made up of little segments called drooplets, and the blackberry is only fully ripe when these are soft. They should also be black all over without a hint of red or green.

Blackberry and lemon pudding

Not many people expect to find blackberries as they spoon into this pudding. The slight sourness of the berries disappears completely with cooking. Everything about this is soft and sweet.

500g (18oz) blackberries
30g (1¼ oz) butter, softened
125g (4½oz) caster sugar
finely grated zest and juice of 1 lemon

2 medium eggs, separated
150ml (5fl oz) milk
30g (1¼ oz) plain flour

Serves 4

Preheat the oven to 190°C/375°F/Gas 5.

Place the berries in a gratin dish that holds about 600ml (1 pint).

Beat the softened butter with 2 tbsp of the sugar in a medium bowl until very soft and pale. Add the zest and the juice of the lemon. Beat the egg yolks into the milk and gradually add this to the lemon mix, alternating it with the flour and the rest of the sugar, beating all the time. Blend until well mixed.

Beat the egg whites to soft peaks and gently fold them into the creamed mixture.

Pour the creamed mixture evenly over the berries. Set the dish in a roasting tin and pour about 3cm (1¼in) boiling water into the roasting tin.

Bake for about 40–50 minutes, until the pudding is brown and set. When you press the sponge with a finger, if it leaves no impression, the pud is cooked.

Serve hot or cold with whipped cream.

Blackberry vodka

The most difficult part of this is leaving the vodka alone until it's ready. At the time of writing, mine's still sitting in the cupboard waiting. This is a very grown-up way of preserving these late summer and autumn fruits.

1kg (2lb 4oz) blackberries
125g (4½oz) granulated sugar
1 x 75cl bottle vodka

Makes about 1.5 litres (2¾ pints)

Lightly crush the berries and put them into a large, wide-necked jar (at least 2 litres/3½ pints). Pour over the sugar and vodka. Shake the jar and leave in a dark, cool place for a month or so. Be sure to shake the jar every couple of days during this period.

At the end of a month, strain off the berries, using a fine piece of muslin in a sieve. Leave to drain for a couple of hours. Decant the vodka into clean bottles, seal and label. Leave for at least another 2 months in a cool, dark place before drinking.

Blackberry and apple pudding

Nobody can resist a sponge pudding. Serve with cream or custard – it's your choice.

125g (4½oz) cooking apples, peeled, cored
  and sliced
30g (1¼oz) soft brown sugar
125g (4½oz) blackberries
175g (6oz) self-raising flour

a pinch of salt
85g (3oz) shredded suet
55g (2oz) caster sugar
150ml (5fl oz) full-fat milk

Serves 4

Put the apple slices in the bottom of a greased 1.2 litre (2 pint) pudding bowl. Sprinkle with the brown sugar, then top with the berries.

Place the flour, salt, suet and caster sugar in a bowl, and stir until evenly mixed. Add enough of the milk to make a soft dropping consistency. Spoon this mixture over the fruit and level the top of the pudding.

Cover the pudding with a layer of buttered foil with a pleat in it. Tie down with string. Use extra string to make a lifting handle over the pudding. Place the pudding on a trivet or upturned saucer in a large saucepan. Pour in boiling water until the water comes halfway up the pudding bowl.

Bring the water to the boil, reduce to a simmer, cover the saucepan, and steam the pudding for 1½ hours. Make sure the water does not boil dry, and top up with boiling water as needed.

Turn the pudding out of the bowl, and serve.

Winter

Winter ingredients

FISH

BRILL (*see* page 116)

COLEY (*see* page 24)

CRAB (*see* page 70)

HAKE This deep-water fish is a member of the cod family. It has beautiful, very soft, pink-tinged flesh. It has amazingly few bones and they are very easy to remove. If you manage to find one – they are becoming very rare and expensive – handle carefully; the soft flesh just falls apart.

HERRING This fish is plentiful and cheap. It is unmistakable with its blue-black top, silver underbelly and pointy head. Most herring we eat is pickled, but the herring is a very decent fish cooked and eaten fresh (grilled, baked or fried). When fresh, you can lift out the backbone, and most of the other little bones come with it.

JOHN DORY (*see* page 24)

MUSSELS (*see* recipes, pages 174–177) Most of our mussels are cultivated. When you buy, tap two mussels together: they should sound full and meaty and not hollow. Rinse them under cold running water and scrub away any sand or mud. Cut off the ropey bit, and discard any that are damaged. Concentrate on the word 'open'. If any of them are open before you cook them, throw them away. If any of them are not open after you have cooked them, throw them away.

OYSTER (*see* page 116)

SKATE (*see* page 25)

SMOKED HADDOCK (*see* recipes, pages 178–181) The haddock is a smaller member of the cod family. It is now under as much pressure from intensive fishing as its bigger cousin (*see* page 116). Haddock are traditionally smoked over seaweed, 'hot' or 'cold'. The famous 'Arbroath smokie' is a small haddock, hot-smoked over peat.

SPRAT (*see* page 117)

WHITEBAIT Bit of a problem this, because the whitebait isn't actually one fish at all. It is lots of very small fish, normally sprats or herrings. They are only about 5cm (2in) long so you should eat them whole. Roll in seasoned flour, deep-fry and serve with lemon.

WHITING This is a tiny little member of the cod family, which is delicate in flesh as well as in flavour. They are far too small to fillet and neither are they strong enough to be grilled. Gentle poaching is the best bet for cooking it, and it's good in soups or fishcakes.

GAME

GROUSE (*see* recipes, pages 172–173) This bird is a real luxury item, and never cheap. It has dark red, rich, gamey flesh, but the flavour is unusual, almost bitter, with a herby undertone that comes from the heather diet. Two good things about the grouse are that, firstly, it's a perfect one-portion size, and, secondly, that it doesn't need to be hung; it can be eaten 24 hours after it's been shot.

VENISON (*see* recipes, pages 168–171) Venison can come from any member of the deer family, and can include reindeer, elk or antelope. Some venison is wild, some is farmed, and you can get hold of park deer: ask your butcher which. Either way, it has dense, dark red meat, with very little fat. Because it doesn't have much fat, venison tends to dry quickly. Add moisture when cooking by using pork or bacon fat. Sharp and sweet flavours, such as redcurrants or cranberry, are great accompaniments to venison.

VEGETABLES

BEETROOT (*see* page 117 and *see* recipes, pages 146–149)

BRUSSELS SPROUTS The Brussels sprout is a Brassica, a type of cabbage. Don't eat sprouts until you have frost. Something in the sprouts' make-up reacts well to frost, and heightens their flavour incredibly. It's fair to say that they're not everyone's cup of tea, and it's a tricky job to get kids to eat them. My advice is to purée them with cream and something sweet to disguise the bitterness that young palates hate.

BRUSSELS TOPS Brussels sprouts grow up and down and around a large pole or stem. On the top of this is the top of the plant, the Brussels top. This top forms into a soft-leaved type of small cabbage, similar in texture to a spring green, with the flavour a mix of spring green and Brussels sprout.

CABBAGE (*see* recipes, pages 194–195) There are two main types of cabbage in the Brassica family: kales, whose leaves are spear shaped and grow upwards and outwards from a main stem; and 'headed' cabbages. The latter are cabbages with much thinner leaves, that form and wrap themselves around each other into a ball or 'head'. White, red and Savoy cabbages are all headed cabbages.

White cabbage is crisp and can be cooked, but its main usage is raw in coleslaw. The red cabbage gives us much-needed colour during the winter months, whether raw or cooked. Its neutral flavour allows it to be accompanied by other flavours, like exotic spices, or sometimes fruit. The Savoy cabbage is very popular among professional chefs. It has dark green, rubbery to the touch, wrinkled leaves. At its best, it is deeply flavoured. It is also very hardy and will stand up to a lot of cooking.

CARDOON (*see* page 118)

CARROT (*see* recipes, pages 186–189; *see also* Baby Carrot, page 71, and recipes, pages 96–97) The carrot is the most cultivated root vegetable on the planet. The winter carrot has a stronger flavour than its early-season counterparts, and can stand up to stews and soups. Compared with most root veg, carrots are wonderfully sweet. Try to buy carrots with the ferns attached. The ferns are the first bit to rot, so if the fern is intact you know the carrot is fresh.

CAVOLO NERO For some reason we now know this wonderful kale by its Italian name, 'cavolo nero', meaning black cabbage. It has dark blue-black leaves that are thick, rubbery and wrinkled, lying each side of a central and agreeably slim stem.

CELERIAC Celeriac is not actually a root vegetable, but a swollen stem that sits above the root. It may look ferocious, but its flavour is relatively gentle: a hint of celery and a hint of sweetness. Peeling it can be troublesome. I wouldn't attempt peeling the whole at once: cut off a chunk and peel that.

CELERY Unfortunately many of us never get celery with all its foliage intact. Green celery leaves are fantastic in stocks and can even be chopped up and thrown through salads. Raw, celery is the perfect dipper, a long-handled natural implement for dipping in sauces. With a little salt-a-sprinkled, it is a perfect accompaniment for cheese.

I don't think people cook celery enough. It is one of my favourite vegetables to braise, either in vegetable or meat stocks.

HORSERADISH (*see* page 118)

JERUSALEM ARTICHOKE Jerusalem artichokes are a root or tuber (not a thistle like the globe artichoke). They have a marvellous earthy flavour with a tad of sweetness at the same time. Their flesh is a lovely ivory colour, which discolours very quickly after peeling. If you have trouble peeling away the hard knobbly skins, boil the artichokes first – I recommend 6–8 minutes – and then peel.

LEEK (*see* recipes, pages 196–199) The leek is an allium, a member of the onion family. In fact, whenever a recipe calls for an onion, you can happily replace it with a leek. I think a leek is easier to handle than an onion; it doesn't have an outer skin, it's not wet and slippery, and it doesn't make your eyes sting. The only difficulty is in cleaning it. Because the leek is made up of many layers, somehow bits of grit manage to travel two-thirds of the way down to the middle layer. My advice is to make a slit lengthways down the leek when washing. If you're going to cut into rings, give all these rings a quick shower in a colander.

MUSHROOMS (see page 26)

ONIONS (see page 26)

PARSNIP (see recipes, pages 190–193) Parsnips taste a lot better once we've had a frost, as a chemical reaction heightens the flavour dramatically. Parsnips are very sweet, and before voyages brought sugar back from the New World, parsnips were one of our major sweeteners.

POTATOES (see recipes, pages 182–185; see also New and salad potatoes, page 26 and recipes, pages 60–63) Potatoes do different jobs and this is important. You won't get great chips or fluffy mash if you get the wrong potato. There are all-rounders that will do a decent enough job, I suppose, but if you take your food seriously, it's worth shopping for the correct type.

A good chipper is a starchy potato; a good masher is a fluffy or floury potato. There is a bigger problem searching for good chippers, than mashers, boilers or bakers. The problem is with storage. A chipping potato will not do the job well all year round. While the potatoes are in storage, the starch turns to sugar, resulting in that awful caramelization of your chip in the pan. Just when you think you have found the perfect variety, the next batch you sample will not be so good. My advice is to change your variety throughout the year. Supermarkets are getting better, and now label their spuds, 'best for...'.

All Rounders Maris Piper, King Edward, Cara, Romano.

Bakers Any of the boilers, Aaron, King Edward.

Boilers Bintje, Cyprus, Estima.

Chippers Bintje, Cyprus, Kipfler, Arran Pilot, Ausonia, Spunta, Home Guard, Maris Bard.

Mashers Golden Wonder, Wilja, Pentland Dell, Marfona.

Roasters Cara, Désirée.

SALSIFY (see page 119)

SHALLOTS (see page 27)

SPROUTING BROCCOLI (see page 27 and recipes, pages 54–55)

SWEDE Great value for money, the swede, with tons of good weather-hardy flesh. Roasted or mashed, it's one of the finer things of winter. The swede isn't actually a root, it's the swollen base of a stem, closely related to the turnip.

SWISS CHARD (see page 74 and see recipes, pages 86–89)

TURNIP These come as big as tennis balls, or as small as ping-pong balls. Usually the smaller they are, the sweeter they are. What I didn't realize until recently is how good they are raw. They have a very agreeable crunch and a pepperiness to rival rocket.

Turnips don't have to be pearly white, but they need to be firm. Squeeze them, and there should be virtually no give.

WINTER SQUASH The difference between a winter and summer squash is the thickness of the skin. Winter squashes have very thick, inedible skins, but the flesh inside can be stunning. They come in various shapes and sizes and a myriad of colours. Four varieties I want to draw your attention to are Delicata, Hubbard, Kabocha and Onion.

FRUIT

APPLE (see page 119 and recipes, pages 150–153)

PEAR (see recipes, pages 200–203) There are over 5,000 varieties of European pear. Three quality varieties are regularly available. The big, bulbous, rounded Comice pear reminds me of a pert, sexy

bottom. It's full of juice and a touch grainy, but never unpleasantly so. The useful Conference pear, although round at the bottom, tapers to a point, giving it a conical shape. Heavily scented, a ripe Williams pear will hit your nose from 50 paces. All pears will ripen perfectly at home.

RHUBARB (*see* page 27 and recipes, pages 64–67)

SALADS

CHICORY (*see* page 28)

WATERCRESS (*see* page 120)

HERBS

MINT (*see* page 121)

ROSEMARY (*see* page 121)

SAGE (*see* page 121)

THYME (*see* page 121)

NUTS

HAZELNUT There is confusion as to the difference between the hazelnut, cob and filbert. The name 'filbert' was once applied to very big hazelnuts. Nowadays it's just another name, as is 'cob', although sometimes 'cobnut' applies to very fresh hazelnuts (when they have green husks with wet, milky kernels inside).

Eat hazelnuts in the hand, or toast them in a dry pan for more flavour. They can be ground for baking, or crumble toppings, or even used to thicken sauces. You can chop or grate them to add to stuffing for chicken. Once the kernels are out of their shells, keep them in an airtight container, otherwise they will turn bitter.

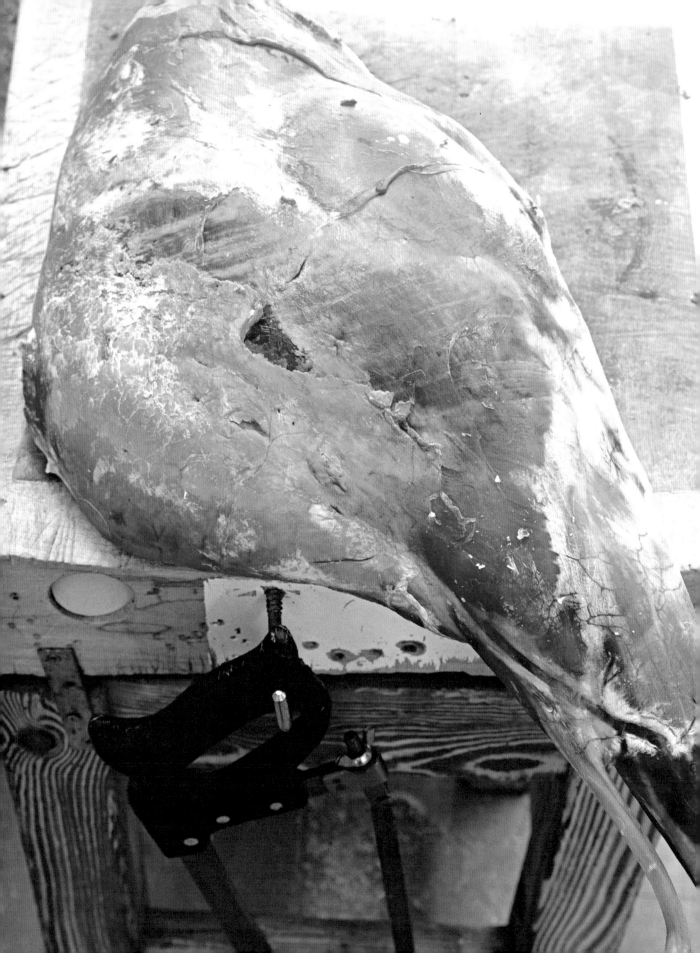

Venison

An older animal needs long, slow cooking and a younger one will cook quicker. The way to tell the difference between old and young butchered venison is by the colour of the scant fat. Young fat is white; older fat is more yellow.

Venison pie

You have to let the meat marinate overnight, and you'll get the best results if you then leave the cooked pie filling overnight as well. When you pull it out of the oven and slice it, you will know why you went to the trouble.

1kg (2¼ lb) stewing venison, cubed
150ml (5fl oz) red wine
6 tbsp vegetable oil
2 bay leaves
3 juniper berries, crushed in a pestle and mortar
5 thyme sprigs
12 small shallots, peeled
1 tbsp plain flour

250ml (9fl oz) beef stock
2 tsp mild mustard
salt and pepper
1 tbsp redcurrant jelly
300g (10½ oz) chestnut mushrooms, quartered
500g (18oz) puff pastry
1 medium egg, beaten

Serves 6

Place the venison in a large bowl with the wine, 2 tbsp of the oil, the bay leaves, juniper berries and 3 sprigs of the thyme. Cover and leave to marinate overnight in a refrigerator.

Preheat the oven to 170°C/325°F/Gas 3. Heat 2 tbsp of the oil in a large frying pan over a medium heat. Add the shallots and fry until browned on all sides, about 5 minutes. Place in a casserole. Drain the meat, reserving the marinade, and dry with kitchen paper. Fry the venison in the same pan and fat, over a high heat, in batches until the meat is browned all over, about another 5 minutes or so. Add to the casserole.

Add the flour to the pan and stir for 2 minutes. Add the marinade, stirring, then add the stock and mustard. Bring to the boil and season. Pour the sauce over the meat. Cover and place in the oven for 1½ hours. Remove from the oven and stir in the redcurrant jelly. Put back in the oven for a further 20 minutes on 200°C/400°F/Gas 6.

Heat the remaining 2 tbsp oil in a large frying pan over a medium-high heat. Fry the mushrooms for about 4 minutes, then add to the casserole with the rest of the thyme. Stir and leave to cool. Check the seasoning. When ready to cook and serve, preheat the oven to 220°C/425°F/Gas 7.

Place the meat in a large pie dish. Roll out the puff pastry on a floured surface until larger than the pie dish. From around the rolled-out pastry cut a 2.5cm (1in) wide strip. Brush the pie dish edge with water and press the cut-out strips on to the edge of the dish. Brush the pastry strips with more water and cover with the rolled-out pastry. Press the pastry down well on the rim to seal. With a sharp knife, cut off the edges of the pastry from the dish. Decorate, if you wish, with pastry offcuts and brush with beaten egg to glaze.

Bake for about 30 minutes until the pastry has risen and is golden brown.

Fruity venison stew

Stews are just lovely. It's as simple as that. The success of combining fruity and gamey flavours is well known. This stew brings them together in a fine manner.

1 knob butter
2 tbsp vegetable oil
1 onion, peeled and chopped
2 celery stalks, chopped
1 tbsp plain flour
2 tsp ground allspice
salt and pepper

800g (1¾ lb) stewing venison, cubed
225g (8oz) fresh cranberries (or frozen)
juice and finely grated zest of 1 orange
300ml (10fl oz) beef stock
400ml (14fl oz) stout or ale

Serves 4

Melt the butter and 1 tbsp of the oil in a large pan over a medium heat. Add the onion and celery and sweat gently for 6 minutes. Remove the vegetables from the pot.

Mix the flour, allspice and salt and pepper in a large bag. Add the cubes of venison and shake the bag. Remove the cubes from the bag: they should be covered with flour. Add the remaining oil to the used pan and heat over quite a high heat. Add the cubes of meat in batches, making sure not to crowd the pan. Brown the meat on all sides.

Return the meat to the pan with the vegetables, cranberries, orange zest and juice. Season, add the stock and beer, and bring to the boil. Reduce to a simmer, cover and cook for at least 45 minutes, or until the meat is tender. Check the seasoning before serving.

Peppered venison steaks

In a book with this many recipes there are always going to be some outright winners. This is one of them.

1 tsp black peppercorns
2 tsp green peppercorns in brine
4 venison steaks
a pinch of salt
a knob of butter

1 tbsp vegetable oil
4 tbsp brandy
1 tbsp redcurrant jelly
4 tbsp crème fraîche

Serves 4

Mix the peppercorns together, then smash them to bits in a pestle and mortar. Spread out on a plate. Cover the steaks evenly with the pepper. Sprinkle with a little salt.

Heat a large frying pan over a medium-high heat. Add the butter and oil. Fry the steaks to your taste. Pour the brandy in the pan, and when warmed up, tip the pan to catch the gas flame (or use a match). When the flames subside, remove the steaks from the pan and keep in a warm place for 10 minutes.

Melt the redcurrant jelly in the pan, then swirl in the crème fraîche and let the juices bubble for a minute to reduce slightly. Serve the sauce with the steaks when they have rested.

Grouse

You only want to roast a young bird, as a grouse over one year old is better for a pie or a stew. The way to tell the age of your bird is to have a very good look at it, and a good feel. Young birds have soft flexible beaks; their feet are also flexible, with no gnarling. Also, the head will have a little bit of give. Make sure you check the wings, as for partridge (*see* page 117).

These birds can dry out dangerously quickly. A nice jacket of bacon and regular basting while cooking is the answer.

Fruit-stuffed grouse

I think a lot of people are scared of these little birds. There's no need to be. Read this carefully; it's not difficult. The flavour of the fruit adds to the bird as does the lovely sweetness of the Marsala.

salt and pepper
4 large Savoy cabbage leaves
2 grouse
juice of ½ lemon
55g (2oz) butter
2 tbsp finely chopped shallot

1 small cooking apple, peeled, cored and chopped
1 pear, peeled, cored and chopped
2 plums, halved, stoned and chopped
a large pinch of mixed spice
50ml (2fl oz) Marsala

Serves 2

Bring a pan of salted water to the boil, add the cabbage leaves and blanch for 3 minutes. Drain well.

Wash the birds and dry on kitchen paper. Sprinkle over the lemon juice and season with salt and pepper. Melt half the butter in a flameproof casserole over a medium heat. Add the grouse and brown well all over. Remove from the casserole.

Add the shallot to the casserole and cook until softened but not browned. Add the fruit and mixed spice and cook for about 5 minutes, until the fruit is just starting to soften.

Use the hot fruit mix to stuff the cavities of the birds. Tie the legs together with kitchen string. Smear the remaining butter over the birds and wrap in the blanched cabbage leaves. Put the wrapped birds back in the casserole. Pour in the Marsala and bring to a simmer. Cover tightly and simmer very gently for 20 minutes, turning halfway through the cooking time, until the birds are tender and cooked through.

Leave the birds to rest for at least 10 minutes before serving.

Mussels

(see also page 164). Mussels manage to be sweet, salty, melt-in-the-mouth and chewy all at the same time – how do they do that? They are a mollusc with pretty blue-black shells. As shellfish go, they are rather good value. All shellfish are sold on weight and the mussel has one of the best meat-to-shell weight ratios.

Garlic-stuffed mussels

Everybody loves mussels. A spoonful of crunchy breadcrumbs full of lemon zest gives them a completely new dimension in this recipe.

2kg (4½lb) mussels
200ml (7fl oz) white wine
4 tbsp finely chopped shallot
125g (4½oz) butter, softened
3 garlic cloves, peeled and crushed
finely grated zest of 2 lemons
2 tbsp chopped parsley leaves

1 tbsp chopped tarragon leaves
1 tbsp finely chopped chives
salt and pepper
125g (4½oz) fresh white breadcrumbs
lemon wedges, to serve

Serves 4

Scrub the mussels well under cold water, and pull off any hairy bits. Discard any that are even slightly open and do not close when tapped against the side of the sink, or damaged. Put in a large pan with the wine and shallot, cover, bring to the boil and cook for about 4–5 minutes, until the mussels have all opened. Drain, keeping the cooking liquid. Discard any mussels that have not opened.

When cool enough to handle, discard the empty half of each shell, placing the shells with a mussel in a large roasting tin.

Pour the reserved cooking liquid into a small pan and boil until reduced to about 3 tbsp. Remove from the heat and cool.

Mix the softened butter with the cooled shallot mixture. Mix in the garlic, lemon zest and herbs, and season. Chill until firm.

Preheat the grill to the highest setting and position the shelf about 10cm (4in) away from the heat.

Share the chilled butter between the mussel shells, then sprinkle with the breadcrumbs. Grill the mussels until the butter is bubbling and the breadcrumbs are crisp. Serve with wedges of lemon.

Mussels in a cream sauce

Mussels are great in a bit of a sauce. This sauce, flavoured with herbs, shallots and wine, is subtle enough to let the mussels have a voice of their own.

1kg (2¼ lb) mussels
250ml (9fl oz) white wine
20g (¾ oz) butter
1 bay leaf
3 parsley stalks
1 sprig thyme

3 tbsp finely chopped shallot
100ml (3½ fl oz) single cream
2 tbsp chopped parsley leaves
salt and pepper

Serves 2

Scrub the mussels under cold water and pull off any hairy bits. Discard any that are even slightly open and do not close when tapped against the side of the sink, or damaged.

Put the mussels in a large pan with the wine, butter, herbs and shallot. Cover, bring to the boil and cook for about 4–5 minutes, until the mussels have all opened. Drain, keeping the cooking liquid. Discard any mussels that have not opened. Discard the herbs.

Place the cooked mussels in two serving bowls and keep warm. Return the cooking liquid to the pot and boil rapidly until slightly thickened. Now pour in the cream with the parsley and cook gently until the sauce has thickened further. Taste for seasoning.

Pour over the mussels and serve straightaway with lots of good bread.

Smoked haddock (*see also* page 164). Smoked haddock is

fantastic in pies, soups or chowders, or even lightly poached in milk with a sticky poached egg perched on top.

Smoked haddock pancakes

These are lovely, if a bit tricky. Everybody should know how to make good pancakes. Once you see these rolled pancakes in a baking tray with the cheese sauce bubbling across the top, you'll know why you put in the effort.

PANCAKES
115g (4oz) plain flour
a pinch of salt
1 medium egg, beaten
2 tbsp melted butter, plus extra for frying
300ml (10fl oz) milk

FILLING
900g (2lb) smoked haddock fillets
1 bay leaf
1 onion, peeled and sliced
5 black peppercorns

600ml (1 pint) milk
450g (1lb) fresh spinach, cooked, drained
    and chopped

SAUCE
about 285ml (9½fl oz) milk
75g (2¾oz) butter
75g (2¾oz) plain flour
salt and pepper
½ tsp grated nutmeg
175g (6oz) Gruyère, grated

Serves 4

Mix the pancake ingredients together in the order given, beating in the liquid slowly to give a smooth batter. Brush a frying pan with butter, heat over a medium heat and pour in enough mixture to cover the pan base. When bubbles start showing, turn the pancake over to cook through. Put the cooked pancake on a plate, cover with a tea-towel, and keep making pancakes until the batter is used up. This should make about 10–12 pancakes. Set aside.

Preheat the oven to 190°C/375°F/Gas 5.

Put the fish in a pan with the bay, onion and peppercorns. Pour over the milk so it just covers the fish. Bring to the boil slowly and simmer for 4 minutes. Take off the heat, drain the fish, reserving the milk, and leave both to cool.

To make the sauce, make the reserved and strained fishy milk up to 850ml (1½ pints) with the fresh milk. Melt the butter in a small pan over a low heat. Add the flour and stir for 2 minutes, gradually adding the milk, stirring all the time to prevent lumps. Bring to the boil and simmer for a couple of minutes until the sauce is smooth and thick. Season with salt, pepper and nutmeg. Stir in the cheese.

When the fish is cool enough to handle, flake it into a bowl, discarding all the bones and skin. Add the chopped spinach, mix and add about a third of the cheese sauce. Check the seasoning.

Divide the filling between the pancakes and roll them up. Place them in a buttered gratin dish (or four individual ones). Cover with the remaining cheese sauce. Bake for about 20 minutes, until bubbling.

Kedgeree

I always look at this dish before I cook it and think it's too wet and it won't work. The rice swallows up the milk amazingly quickly, and you should always keep a watchful eye that it doesn't burn.

5 tbsp vegetable oil
3 onions, peeled, 1 chopped, 2 thinly sliced
salt and pepper
500g (18oz) smoked haddock fillets
1 dried red chilli
300ml (10fl oz) full-fat milk
1 tbsp curry powder

4 cardamom pods, split
1 cinnamon stick, broken into small bits
280g (10oz) basmati rice
55g (2oz) butter
2 medium eggs, freshly hard-boiled
3 tbsp chopped parsley leaves

Serves 4

Heat 2 tbsp of the oil in a large frying pan. Add the sliced onion with a pinch of salt. Fry over a medium heat, stirring occasionally, for about 20 minutes, until golden. Spread on kitchen paper and leave to drain and crisp up.

Place the fish in a medium pan with the chilli and cover with the milk. Bring to a simmer, cover, take off the heat and leave to sit for 10 minutes.

Heat the remaining oil in a large frying pan. Add the chopped onion, curry powder, cardamon pods and cinnamon and fry for about 8 minutes, until soft and golden.

Drain the milk from the fish. Flake the fish carefully to remove the skin and any bones and set aside. Measure the cooking milk and make up to 600ml (1 pint) with water.

Rinse the rice in warm water in a sieve, drain well and stir into the chopped onions. Stir for a couple of minutes to make sure the rice is coated with oil. Pour in the milk, mix, season, cover and simmer gently for 10 minutes, until the rice is tender and all the liquid has been absorbed. Put the butter on top of the cooked rice, then lay the fish on top. Cover again and take off the heat.

When the hard-boiled eggs are cool enough to handle, take off the shells and quarter. Put the eggs on top of the fish and rice, then sprinkle with parsley and the crisp brown onions.

Potatoes (*see also* page 166). I want to take my hat off to this most versatile of foodstuffs. Many times I've been asked for my favourite vegetable and I think many people are surprised when I tell them it's the humble potato. But can you imagine a world without chips or mash?

Potato and sausage hash

What a brilliant breakfast or brunch this is. With the eggs on the top of the pan it just looks yummy. This is also the first and last time I will suggest Daddie's sauce as an accompaniment.

600g (1lb 5oz) large potatoes, peeled and cubed
salt and pepper
2 knobs butter
2 tbsp vegetable oil
2 large onions, peeled and chopped
4 good sausages

250g (9oz) back bacon, chopped
2 tbsp chopped parsley leaves
4 very fresh medium eggs

Serves 4

Bring a pan of salted water to the boil. Add the potatoes and cook for about 4–5 minutes, until only just cooked. Drain well.

Melt half the butter with half the oil in a frying pan over a medium heat. Add the cubed potatoes and fry them gently, until golden brown all over, stirring frequently.

In another frying pan, melt the remaining butter and oil over a medium heat and add the onion. Fry until soft and golden, about 10 minutes.

Add the cooked onions to the crisp potatoes. Using the onion pan fry the sausages and bacon until cooked through, 3–4 minutes. There should be enough oil left in the pan, but if not add a little more.

Cut the sausages up into rings and add them, with the bacon, to the potatoes. Stir in the parsley and season well. Keep warm.

Put about 7.5cm (3in) water in a large frying pan. Bring to the boil, then reduce to a simmer. Break an egg into a cup and carefully pour the egg into the water. Try to do this where the bubbles are just breaking through the water. Poach the egg for about 3 minutes with the water barely simmering. When cooked, remove from the water with a slotted spoon. Keep warm. Repeat one by one with the rest of the eggs.

Drain the eggs well and serve on top of the hash.

Cheesy potato puffs

These are really clever. They rise up like little soufflés. This is something new for your roast dinner.

500g (18oz) potatoes, peeled and cubed
salt and pepper
4 spring onions, finely sliced
55g (2oz) mature Cheddar, finely grated
30g (1¼ oz) butter, plus extra for greasing

3 tbsp milk
freshly grated nutmeg
2 medium eggs, separated

Serves 6

Preheat the oven to 220°C/425°F/Gas 7. Grease a six-hole muffin tin with butter, also greasing the bits between the holes.

Put the potatoes into a medium saucepan and cover with salted water. Bring to the boil and simmer for about 15 minutes, until they are very soft but not breaking up. Drain well. Return to the pan and mash really well.

Mix the onions and cheese with the potatoes. Melt the butter and milk together, and stir into the spuds. Season well with salt, pepper and freshly grated nutmeg, then beat in the egg yolks. Whisk the egg whites to form soft peaks, then gently fold into the potato mixture.

Spoon the mix into the muffin tins and bake for about 15 minutes, until well risen and golden brown.

Carrots

Carrots (*see also* page 163). Carrots come in many colours: purple, yellow, white, red and orange. They also come in many shapes. But shape and colour make no real difference to flavour. If you can't find carrots with ferns on, watch out for discolouring or sponginess to the touch. A good carrot should be firm, bright and erect. What about the old wives' tale about carrots helping you see in the dark? Well, they're packed with vitamin A, which is essential for good optics.

Carrots braised with leeks

As a grower and lover of vegetables, I'm always keen to raise them above the level of a side dish or an afterthought. I love to take time with them, combine them, and add new levels of flavour.

70g (2½oz) butter
700g (1lb 9oz) carrots, peeled and thickly sliced
5 tbsp water
2 fresh bay leaves
salt and pepper

700g (1lb 9oz) leeks, cleaned and cut into
  5cm (2in) lengths
125ml (4fl oz) white wine
2 tbsp chopped tarragon

Serves 6

Heat 25g (1oz) of the butter in a medium pan, add the carrots and cook gently for 5 minutes. Add the water and bay leaves, and season. Bring to the boil and cook for about 10 minutes, until the carrots are cooked. If there is any liquid left in the pan, raise the heat and boil off all excess liquid. Set aside.

Heat another 25g (1oz) of butter in a large frying pan and add the leeks in a single layer. Fry gently for 5 minutes over a medium heat, turning halfway through. Do not allow to brown. Season.

Add the wine and half the tarragon to the leeks, cover the pan and cook for another 5 minutes, until the leeks are cooked through. Again, increase the heat to boil off most of the excess liquid (without a lid), leaving a couple of tablespoons of juice.

Add the carrots to the leeks and heat gently, adding the rest of the butter. Serve with the rest of the tarragon scattered over the vegetables.

Carrot and dill soup

Add this one to your soup repertoire. It's full of flavour and, with the dill on top, I think it looks very pretty.

85g (3oz) butter
400g (14oz) carrots, peeled and sliced
1 large onion, peeled and sliced
1 large potato, peeled and thinly sliced

700ml (1¼ pints) vegetable or chicken stock
2 tbsp chopped dill, plus 4 extra sprigs for garnish
salt and pepper

Serves 4

Melt the butter in a large pan over a medium heat. Add the carrot and onion, and sweat gently for 5 minutes. Add the potato, cover and sweat for a further 10 minutes. Now add the stock and the chopped dill, and season. Bring to the boil, reduce to a simmer and cook for 30 minutes.

Purée the soup using a stick blender, leaving some lumps for texture.

Before serving, check the seasoning and garnish each bowl with a sprig of dill.

Winter carrot salad

Winter and salad are not words you often hear in the same sentence. This is a shame, I think. We can turn root vegetables into something light and refreshing, and this is a perfect example.

1kg (2¼ lb) carrots, peeled and coarsely grated
3 tbsp orange-blossom water
2 tbsp finely chopped mint
2 garlic cloves, peeled and crushed
1 tsp caster sugar

1 tsp lemon juice
5 tbsp good olive oil
salt and pepper

Serves 6

Place the grated carrots in a large bowl. Add the remaining ingredients and stir well.

Check the seasoning and leave for at least 10 minutes before serving.

Parsnips

(see also page 166). Be careful when you peel parsnips, as a lot of the flavour lies just under the skin. Be careful, too, when you're cooking them, as obviously the thin end is going to cook a lot quicker than the fat end. It's best to cook the fat bits before the thin bits.

Parsnip croquettes

These are clever little things, all soft on the inside and a bit crispy outside. In fact, they're just like a potato croquette, but with the parsnip's sweetness. Eat with any cooked meat.

450g (1lb) parsnips, peeled and chopped
salt and pepper
30g (1¼oz) butter
1 garlic clove, peeled and crushed
1 x 100g (3½oz) pack peeled whole chestnuts

1 tbsp chopped parsley leaves
1 medium egg, beaten
55g (2oz) fresh white breadcrumbs
vegetable oil, for deep-frying

Serves 4

Put the parsnips in a pan, cover with salted water, and bring to the boil. Cover and simmer for about 15–20 minutes, until soft. Drain well and place in a bowl.

Melt the butter in a small pan, add the garlic and cook for a few seconds. Add the parsnip and mash well. Mash the chestnuts well and add to the parsnip mixture along with the parsley and some seasoning. Mix well.

Heat some oil in a suitable pan ready for deep-frying.

Form about 1 tbsp of the parsnip mixture into a croquette shape. Dip each croquette in beaten egg, then into the breadcrumbs to coat.

Drop each croquette into the hot oil – don't overcrowd the pan – and deep-fry for 3–4 minutes, until golden and crisp. Drain on kitchen paper before serving.

Parsnip and steak pie

This is a truly fantastic pie, and is easy to make. Just wait until you slice through the light pastry and smell the filling. The slow cooking makes the parsnip slices wonderfully soft.

2 tbsp vegetable oil
30g (1¼ oz) butter
1kg (2¼ lb) stewing steak, cubed
1 large onion, peeled and thinly sliced
2 tbsp plain flour
450ml (16fl oz) beef stock
300ml (10fl oz) dry cider
2 tsp chopped thyme leaves

1 tsp ground allspice
salt and pepper
450g (1lb) parsnips, peeled and thickly sliced
450g (1lb) carrots, peeled and thickly sliced
350g (12oz) puff pastry
1 medium egg, beaten

Serves 6

Preheat the oven to 180°C/350°F/Gas 4.

Heat the oil and butter in a large frying pan over a medium-high heat. Add the meat in batches and fry until brown all over. Put the browned meat into a large casserole. Lower the heat under the pan, add the onion and fry until softened, about 5 minutes. Add the flour to the onion, stir and fry for a couple of minutes. Add the stock to the pan, stirring all the time, and bring to the boil. Add the cider, thyme, allspice and some salt and pepper. Bring to the boil then pour the sauce over the meat. Braise in the oven for 1 hour.

In the meantime, bring a large pan of salted water to the boil. When boiling, add the parsnips and carrots, and blanch for 3 minutes. Drain well.

After the casserole has been cooking for an hour, remove from the oven and add the drained vegetables. Stir and return to the oven for another hour, until the meat and vegetables are tender. Remove from the oven and leave to cool. Check the seasoning.

When ready to cook and serve, increase the oven temperature to 220°C/425°F/Gas 7.

Put the cold meat into a suitable pie dish. Cover with pastry and glaze as described on page 169.

Bake for about 30 minutes, until the pastry has risen and is golden brown.

Cabbage

(see also page 165). I used to detest cabbage as a child, yet I love it now. Maybe it's because I cook my own and I cook it gently. The awful smell of boiling cabbage is caused by sulphur from the earth. The cabbage sucks it up, keeps it, then releases it when we cook it for too long.

Braised red cabbage and beetroot

Be sparing with the horseradish if you're not a big fan, but stir in as much as you want if you can handle it.

55g (2oz) butter
2 star anise
2 cinnamon sticks
1 red cabbage, cored and finely sliced
2 red onions, peeled and finely sliced
5 raw beetroots, peeled and thickly sliced
3 tbsp caster sugar

100ml (3½fl oz) red wine vinegar
juice and finely grated zest of 1 orange
salt and pepper
1 cooking apple, peeled, cored and thickly sliced
3 tbsp freshly grated horseradish

Serves 8

Melt the butter in a large pan over a medium heat and fry the spices for a couple of minutes. Tip in the cabbage, onion and beets along with the sugar, vinegar, orange juice and zest. Season and stir. Bring to the boil, reduce to a simmer, cover and cook for about 45 minutes.

Now add the apple, cover again, and cook for another 45 minutes, until the cabbage is nice and soft. Stir in the horseradish and check the seasoning before serving.

Cabbage cooked with gin

It does sound funny, but I promise it's fantastic. You lose the sharp alcohol taste and are left with soft buttery cabbage leaves infused with a light gin flavour. After this, you'll never see a cabbage in the same way again.

1 Savoy cabbage, about 600g (1lb 5oz), trimmed
6 juniper berries
2 garlic cloves, peeled
salt and pepper

55g (2oz) butter, softened
3 tbsp gin

Serves 4

Quarter the cabbage, take out and discard the hard core and finely shred the leaves. Wash them and drain well.

Crush the berries, garlic and salt together in a pestle and mortar until you get a rough paste. Mix into the butter.

Melt this butter in a large saucepan over a lowish heat until it starts to sizzle, then turn up the heat to medium and stir in the cabbage to coat in butter. Add the gin, cover the pan and cook for about 4 minutes, shaking the pan a few times during cooking. The cabbage should still have a crunch. Season with pepper, stir and serve.

Leeks

(*see also* page 165). Remove the top green bits of your leeks before you cook, as they are very bitter and tough. There are Middle Eastern varieties of leek that are green all over and pleasantly mild, but unless you're living there, you are unlikely to see any. So, cut off the green, and then wash carefully (*see* page 166). Baby leeks are a joy. They're tender, slippery and grit-free.

Leek tart

Eat this tart hot, warm or cold. In fact, it's probably best to make two. I found it really difficult not to eat it as soon as it came out of the oven, and was still picking at it the next morning for breakfast.

500g (18oz) leeks, white part only, cleaned
and trimmed
30g (1¼oz) butter
100g (3½oz) streaky bacon, finely chopped
salt and pepper

100g (3½oz) Lancashire cheese, crumbled
2 medium eggs, beaten
1 tbsp crème fraîche
1 packet ready-rolled puff pastry

Serves 4

Preheat the oven to 220°C/425°F/Gas 7.

Slice the leeks into thin rounds. Melt the butter in large pan, add the bacon and fry until the bacon is brown. Now add the leeks to the pan, stir, cover, and cook over a medium heat for about 10 minutes, until the leeks are really soft. Remove from the heat and allow to cool.

Season the cooled leeks well, then mix in the cheese, most of the egg (keep 1 tbsp aside for glazing) and the crème fraiche.

Unroll the pastry on to a baking sheet. Cut a shallow line about 2cm (¾in) in from all four edges. Do not cut all the way through the pastry.

Carefully spread the leek mixture evenly on to the pastry within the cut lines. Use the rest of the egg to brush on to the edges of the pastry.

Bake for about 30 minutes, until puffed up and browned.

Braised leeks and hazelnuts

I've said eight baby leeks here, but I don't know how baby your babies are! If they're really small you will probably need more. I like the crunch on top of the leeks with this one.

8 small baby leeks, trimmed
55g (2oz) butter
55g (2oz) fresh white breadcrumbs

55g (2oz) shelled hazelnuts, toasted and
   coarsely chopped
salt and pepper

Serves 4

Wash the leeks really well, making a slit down the side of each leek on the green part only to rinse out any dirt. Cut them in half.

Melt 40g (1½oz) of the butter in a medium frying pan over a medium heat. Add the breadcrumbs and fry until golden brown, stirring all the time. Stir in the nuts, and season. Take off the heat and keep aside.

Put the leeks into a pan large enough to take them all in one layer. Add 3 tbsp water and the rest of the butter and season. Bring to the boil, reduce to a simmer, cover, and cook for about 15 minutes, until the leeks are tender.

Remove the lid when the leeks are cooked and boil away any excess juices, just leaving the butter. Sprinkle with the crisp breadcrumb mixture to serve.

Baked leeks

I have a real soft spot for things baking in the oven, especially vegetables. We do too much boiling and serving, and not enough slow cooking with sauce.

8 small leeks, about 700g (1lb 9oz), trimmed
salt and pepper
2 medium eggs, beaten
150g (5½oz) goat's cheese, crumbled

6 tbsp Greek yoghurt
55g (2oz) Parmesan, finely grated
30g (1¼oz) fresh white breadcrumbs

Serves 4

Preheat the oven to 180°C/350°F/Gas 4.

Wash the leeks really well, making a slit down the side of each leek on the green part only to rinse out any dirt.

Bring a large pan of salted water to the boil. Drop in the leeks and simmer for about 8 minutes, until soft. Remove the leeks from the water with a large spoon and drain well. Arrange in a gratin dish which just holds the leeks in a single layer.

Beat the eggs with the goat's cheese, yoghurt and half the Parmesan, and season. Pour this mixture over the leeks. Mix the breadcrumbs and the rest of the Parmesan together with a little seasoning, and scatter all over the sauced leeks.

Bake for about 40 minutes, until golden brown.

Pears

I've been surrounded by good fruit all of my working life but still, to this day, I cannot resist a ripe pear. When I get to the farm these days, it's the first thing that I reach for. I still love to gorge myself silly on them as they're so juicy. They give sweetness, quench thirst, and wash the palate all at the same time. They are also perfect when cooked. A pear poached in red or white wine is a very fine thing indeed. If you have money to spare, nothing beats a pear poached in a good dessert wine. The pear has a perfect affinity with cream, chocolate and, in a salad, with blue cheese.

Pear and apple crumble

Everybody should learn how to make a crumble. Once you know how, you can use any fruit you like, but start with my pear and apple and I promise you won't be disappointed.

2 large ripe dessert pears, peeled, cored and chopped
1 Bramley cooking apple, peeled, cored and chopped
1 crisp eating apple, peeled, cored and chopped
1 tbsp lemon juice
5 tbsp light brown sugar

150g (5½oz) plain flour
100g (3½oz) butter, cold and cubed
55g (2oz) shelled hazelnuts, toasted and chopped
2 tbsp rolled oats

Serves 4

Preheat the oven to 180°C/350°F/Gas 4.

Mix the fruit with the lemon juice, then place in a shallow gratin dish. Sprinkle over 4 tbsp of the sugar.

In a food processor, whizz the flour and butter together until the mixture looks like breadcrumbs. Put into a bowl and add the nuts and oats, and finally, the remaining sugar.

Sprinkle the crumble mixture over the fruit and press down lightly with your hands.

Bake for about 35 minutes, until the topping is golden. Allow to stand for at least 10 minutes before serving, or you will burn your mouth on the fruit. It's compulsory to serve this with custard!

Pears in chocolate

Some things just look too good to eat, but eat them you should. Rich sticky chocolate fills your mouth, and the sweet acidity of the beautiful pear rinses your palate clean for the next spoonful.

This dish is made with raw eggs. It is prudent for vulnerable people such as pregnant and nursing mothers, invalids, the elderly, babies and young children to avoid uncooked dishes made with eggs.

4 large ripe dessert pears
15g (½oz) shelled almonds, finely chopped
15g (½oz) glacé cherries, finely chopped
125g (4½oz) good-quality dark chocolate
3 tbsp strong black coffee
30g (1¼oz) butter

2 tbsp rum
2 medium eggs, separated
2 tbsp crème fraîche

Serves 4

Peel the pears thinly, keeping the stems on the fruit. Core the fruit carefully with a teaspoon from its base. Cut a sliver of pear off the base so that the fruit stands upright. Mix together the nuts and cherries and use to stuff the cavities of each pear. Stand the pears upright in one large or four small, shallow serving dishes.

Break up the chocolate and place in a medium bowl with the coffee. Place the bowl over a pan of simmering water, making sure the bottom of the bowl does not touch the water. Stir occasionally until the chocolate has melted. Remove the bowl from the heat. Stir in the butter and then the rum. Beat the egg yolks into the chocolate. Whisk the egg whites to soft peaks and carefully fold them into the chocolate mousse.

Carefully pour this mixture over the pears so they are evenly coated and each pear has its share of mousse.

Chill for at least 3 hours (or overnight, if possible) before serving. Serve each pear accompanied by a blob of crème fraîche.

Index

Thanks to Zed for being there day after day to help with the recipes, and to my girlfriend Panda for putting in hours of typing.